T0271055

The Focused Organization

To all those millions of anonymous project managers who, with their unlimited commitment and drive, have contributed to the generating of value for business, with the ultimate aim of making a better world for all of us.

And yet, the appreciation of the value of their work is often barely acknowledged by senior leaders. I hope this book helps all of them, even if only a little, to get that well deserved recognition.

The Focused Organization

How Concentrating on a Few
Key Initiatives Can Dramatically
Improve Strategy Execution

ANTONIO NIETO-RODRIGUEZ

Routledge
Taylor & Francis Group

LONDON AND NEW YORK

First published 2012 by Ashgate Publishing

2 Park Square, Milton Park, Abingdon, Oxon OX14 4RN
711 Third Avenue, New York, NY 10017, USA

Routledge is an imprint of the Taylor & Francis Group, an informa business

First issued in paperback 2016

British Library Cataloguing in Publication Data
Nieto-Rodriguez, Antonio.
  The focused organization : how concentrating on a few key
  initiatives can dramatically improve strategy execution.
  1. Strategic planning. 2. Project management. 3. Portfolio
  management. 4. Corporate culture. 5. Intellectual capital.
  I. Title
  658.4′012-dc23

ISBN 978-1-4094-2566-3 (hbk)
ISBN 978-1-138-27416-7 (pbk)

Library of Congress Cataloging-in-Publication Data
Nieto-Rodriguez, Antonio.
  The focused organization : how concentrating on a few key initiatives can
  dramatically improve strategy execution / by Antonio Nieto-Rodriguez.
    p. cm.
  Includes bibliographical references and index.
  ISBN 978-1-4094-2566-3 (hbk) -- ISBN 978-1-4094-2567-0 (ebk)
  1. Strategic planning. 2. Project management. I. Title.
  HD30.28.N545 2011
  658.4′012--dc23

2011039671

Contents

List of Figures

List of Tables

About the Author

Image credit: Olivier Melebeck

Antonio Nieto-Rodriguez is an expert in strategy execution and project management. He currently works for BNP Paribas Fortis as Head of Transversal Portfolio Management, which deals with the prioritization, the selection and the execution of all the large strategic projects in the bank (130 approximately). He is former Head of Post Merger Integration at Fortis Bank, where he was involved in the largest merger in the financial service sector, the acquisition of ABN AMBRO. Previously, he worked as a consultant for PricewaterhouseCoopers for more than ten years, where he was the global lead practitioner for the Project and Portfolio Management practice in which he advised many of the top European companies on portfolio management and how to improve their portfolio management practices. In 2004, while working for PwC, he launched the first global survey on project management maturity. This lead to the well-known white paper, 'Boosting Business Performance with Project Management,' which today is used as a basis for many other similar research.

He has an MBA from London Business School and a university degree on Economics. He is fluent in Spanish, English, Dutch, Italian and French. Antonio is also a Professor of Project Management and Strategy Execution in the MBAs of Solvay Business School in Belgium, Nyenrode Business School in the Netherlands and Boston University, USA. He is a regular keynote speaker in conferences on project portfolio management and writer of articles in different project management magazines.

He launched and manages the largest think tank on Strategy Execution in LinkedIn – StrateXecution (http://www.linkedin.com/groups?gid=2548095 &trk=hb_side_g) – with more than 3,500 experts worldwide.

Antonio is a member of the London Business School Belgium alumni board, member of the Project Management Institute Belgian Chapter board and a member of the global Advisory Committee of the Enterprise Management Association International (EMA-I). He also helps the non-profit organization Economistas Sin Fronteras, for which he wrote the book 'Ayudas y subvenciones de la UE para ONG' ('EU grants for NGOs'), edited by UNED, published in 2001.

Foreword

When I reflect back on 2011, I will probably remember it as a year like any other year: big news, small news, and no news, all wrapped into 12 months. October 12, at first, seemed like it was no different than any other morning. I woke up that morning, like every morning since, before dawn to see the sun rise, and breathe in the new day. I follow a routine of coffee and news. However, what made that morning different was that the press was full of information about Apple. Steve Jobs had recently died, and every publication from *The Economist* to local tabloids had obituaries and tributes to this great genius of the technology world. But amid all the tributes was the buzz about his loss to Apple: could Apple survive without him? Was it his genius that made things happen? Did he direct the company and oversee every single major product launch? His funeral had just been held, and the press was on the attack.

It seemed that the press was wrong; it had to be. You see, on that day, the tributes were printed side-by-side with the news of the new iPhone 4S. Only six days after Jobs' death, Apple launched the iPhone 4S … and sold 4.5 million units in the first weekend. Even with the press pining away that it was not the '5,' initial sales were nearly double the number of iPhone 4 models in its first weekend of sales. WOW! Now, you would think that the markets would be excited about this great news, and that the stock would soar. But the opposite occurred. The stock value had steadily fallen since Jobs' death, with confidence in the company on the decline. That 'buzz' I mentioned earlier was not just idle chat. It went to the heart of Apple's ability to survive without ONE man … their 'genius.' Only time will tell what is to become of Apple without Jobs at the helm.

It made me think about all of the companies and executives that I have met around the globe over the last two decades. The truth is that the really successful companies, and they were a minority, were driven through strategy; they incorporated strong, powerful teams to drive strategic change, whether it was opening into a new market, introducing a new product or product line, or restructuring an organization. It was never about one man ... it was about one focus, and that focus was *strategic change*.

I have too many stories of highly-successful government and business leaders alike confirming with me that the truly successful shift occurring in organizations today was a focus on specific results, with the assets of the organizations being aligned to achieve strategic change. Those organizations that did not focus on strategic results struggled, and in many cases failed. Those that did focus on strategic results survived, and in most cases excelled.

This trend wasn't minor; it is happening across the globe. Nor was it limited to the manufacturing sector. For example, the widening of the Panama Canal is an extraordinary example of how the country of Panama has maintained the budget and schedule of one of the most complex projects in the world, in preparation for its grand opening in 2014. Panama recognized that the Canal was its greatest source of revenue and one of the most critical links in the global supply chain. Panama did this through world-class project and program management. In less than four years BMW redesigned all of its car and motorcycle models, introducing new engines, new technologies, opening new plants to produce them. They did all of this while dramatically increasing stock value and sales. Were these achievements about the work of one man, one man directing an entire organization? Hardly! In every case it was all about strategic focus and disciplined project, program and portfolio management.

These organizations were structured and focused along strategic lines. Their resources and human capital were aligned with a clear sense of mission and a sense of urgency that is not lost on any day in any week. And this is what breeds success ... when everyone in the organization is focused on success.

I wish I could say that these successful organizations were universal, that the status of all organizations across the globe were focused only on strategic results and maintained project, program and portfolio management as a core, strategic competency. Unfortunately, I can't say that. Yes it is a trend; that I can confirm. But too much work is left to be done. The university system globally has been slow to respond, and companies have been cautious of major change. But the trends are there, and a set of new strategic management tools need to be continually added to the corporate tool box to help companies excel.

Books are one of these tools. I have been asked to read and comment on many books. And I do this with an eagerness and enjoyment, since I learn and grow by reading and seeing the work of the creative people in the project management community. When Antonio Nieto-Rodriguez asked me to review his book, though hesitant, I was again eager to see if I could learn from him. I not only learned, but resonated on the framework he has built in his book. He shares his experience and research on the FOCUSED organization; it mirrors what I have seen.

His book actually takes two paths. Upfront, he outlines the dilemma of why he feels organizations have not adopted these principles quickly enough. He shares his own experiences and research. And then he takes us on a journey of discovery, where he explains in detail, how successful companies have been winning the competitive battle through intentional strategic planning and change. He brings us through a step-wise analysis from reorganizing and refocusing projects ('less is more' ... fewer projects, driven out of strategy); aligning staff and resources along strategic rather than operational lines; maintaining a sense of urgency while never losing sight of the competition; and always holding the organization accountable for success and performance excellence.

Yes, Antonio is on to something. Personally, I think we have no choice but to read this book and respond to it. Whether you agree with his approach or not is not the issue. You don't really have time to stay within your own world to address today's challenges. Is it a cliché to say that the world is changing in a radically different way, faster and more unpredictably than before? And that we must act more quickly to change? Hardly ... the truth is, we must respond, we must act, and we must act now.

Take a look at the differences that separate our world today from our past. Let's start with delivering value and impact in the highest state of uncertainty since the industrial revolution. The latest global census reminds us that population growth was understated and the planet will reach 10 billion in population by 2050, a planet that cannot deliver the food, water and energy to support its current population. Today, across the globe, our 'new demographic' of early 20 year olds are facing the highest unemployment rate of any similar demographic in the last century, with a fragile, fickled global economy that seems on the brink of disaster every day. Organizational leaders are expected to have impact in a world of paradoxes ... turn on a dime, but do it with fiscal discipline; deliver on the needs before they materialize, but do it with predictable processes; and if it fails, don't take much time to do forensics, but yet be transparent and accountable.

Is this an environment where we should be cautious and hesitant? Or is it time to seek out new ideas, robust ideas, and consider new ways of structuring for success. I, like Antonio, think it is time to change so that we can succeed in a radically different world. The pace is breathtaking, so read, consider, and learn; but above all, we all must ACT, and we must ACT now.

Greg Balestrero

Acknowledgements

I would like to sincerely thank Jonathan Norman from Gower Publishing for believing in my idea and agreeing to publish this book. Thanks also go to my editor, Jill Uhlfelder, who coached me for two years in this incredible experience; Greg Balestrero for writing such an insightful Foreword; Stuart Crainer, Max Wideman, Russell Archibald, and David Pells for their brilliant endorsements; and Adam Guppy for his excellent management of the production process. Lastly, thanks to my wife, children, family, and friends, and to all those people who have supported me in this long journey, you are too numerous to mention here, but you are not forgotten.

Benny's Tale

The year was 1913, and the global economy had begun to recover after a more than decade-long economic crisis. The public sector was pumping money into the economy like never before. Spare Parts Benny, Inc., a spare parts production company founded three years prior by Benny White, with loans of $600, was booming.

Benny started his business in an old hut close to his home, with a team of five workers and one machine that produced spare parts – cylinders and valve gears – for the assembly of trains in the southwestern United States. Because the company was the first in the area to specialize in spare parts, Benny benefited from first-mover advantage. Benny was *extremely focused* on his business, determined to make it a success. He received many orders very quickly, as there was a huge demand to reconstruct the country's infrastructure.

After only two years in the business, Spare Parts Benny, Inc. had more than 200 employees and five production machines. Concurrently, Benny began producing special parts for cars, at that time a new gadget for Americans. The first such vehicle, introduced by the Ford Motor Company on 1 October 1908, was called the Model T.

In the early 1910s, Benny White was one of the most successful businessmen in the United States. Not only had he established six factories throughout the country, employing more than 3,000 people, he was also selling his quality products to customers both in his country and abroad. His turnover had multiplied by 20 since he started his business, with consistent double-growth digits year after year. Benny's ambition was to become one of the largest spare parts producers in the world, a goal that was already within reach …

Read the whole of Benny's Tale and trace the ideas developed in The Focused Organization *through the story of The Evolution of Spare Parts Benny, Inc. on pages 173–212.*

Reviews for
The Focused Organization

These days, for most companies the strategic objective of their CEOs and senior executives is to achieve sustainable growth in the market place and do it cost effectively. In this book, Antonio Nieto-Rodriguez advocates a policy of being singularly focused on the projects that will make the biggest contribution to the organization's vision, strategy and purpose. He examines the conflict between 'run-the-business' (operations) and 'change-the-business' (projects), the optimum balance of resources between the two, and how best to move forward. The key is in adopting 'FOCUSED' as an acronym for: F-Fewer projects, rather than many; O-Organized staff; C-Competitive mind set; U-Urgency; S-Strategic alignment; E-Excellence; and D-Discipline. Adoption of this paradigm shift is not a guarantee of success, but it will certainly reduce the chances of failure.

R. Max Wideman, P.Eng., FICE, FEIC, FCSCE, FPMI, MCMI

The world is awash with business ideas and tools. But what really matters to business leaders is making things happen, execution. That is what they are measured on and what really turns them on. Based on research and extensive experience, The Focused Organization provides new, compelling and highly practical insights into the reality of execution.

Stuart Crainer, Editor, *Business Strategy Review*,
co-creator Thinkers50

This book fills a long-standing need in management literature by presenting, as it does, sound and proven concepts, principles, and practices for translating strategies into results. Nieto-Rodriguez clearly describes the reasons behind the widespread corporate failure to successfully execute strategies, and presents a practical approach for companies and agencies to become his vision of The Focused Organization.

Russell D. Archibald, Honorary Fellow APM/IPMA, PMI Fellow, PMP
and author of *Managing High-Technology Programs and Project*

In his new book, The Focused Organization, Antonio Nietro-Rodriguez brilliantly describes some significant problems in many organizations today and offers a simple yet profound solution – increased focus on those few projects that are most important. He explains how this can be accomplished, using clear examples and practical steps. This is a powerful book that will help many executives and businesses. Outstanding!

David Pells, Managing Editor, *Project Management World*

Introduction

I have always been intrigued by the fact that most companies have very similar strategies and business objectives (e.g., growth, expansion, product innovation, market leadership) but just a few succeed in achieving them. What do these successful companies do differently?

The way in which companies execute their strategy and link it to their portfolio of projects has also been a source of interest to me. In particular, I have been intrigued by the fact that running a large and complex project across an entire organization – e.g., a merger, an international expansion, an initial public offering (IPO), a cost-reduction initiative, a business reengineering or a new system implementation – always seemed to result in missed deadlines, significantly higher costs than estimated and fewer benefits than initially planned.

After serving as manager of numerous strategic and transformational projects, I started to wonder how organizations could successfully select and manage hundreds of projects – some of them large, transformational and strategic, but also lots of smaller ones – when most of them had difficulty efficiently handling just one. I also questioned why none of these companies had linked their vast assortment of projects to their overall corporate strategy. I had the feeling that this was all a big 'black box' and could not understand why management did nothing to take control of such a large amount of company assets and resources.

In searching for an answer, I reviewed old and recent business research papers and spoke with senior executives and academics; however, nothing gave me a satisfactory explanation. Surprisingly, I realized that there was very little literature and academic thought on strategy execution/implementation. That is when I decided to conduct my own research.

First, I wanted to examine the different ways in which companies select and manage their projects and to determine whether certain practices had a positive impact on a company's strategy execution, including its financial growth and shareholder value. Second, I was looking for the magic formula that would enable an organization to configure all of its various elements – e.g., strategy selection, processes, competencies, structure, roles, systems and culture – so that it maximized its success in these areas.

Surprisingly, my research led me in a direction that was not part of my initial list of objectives. I discovered an astonishing trend that has silently affected the way in which business is conducted today and how organizations create value: almost unaware, companies have begun implementing strategic initiatives through projects and project management. I was also surprised to find that this trend renders obsolete some of the most popularly cited theories in business management, such as Porter's value chain, and identifies flaws in the current accounting standards for assessing an organization's fair value.

The Gap between the Old Industrial World and the New Information Age

Up to the late 1970s, an organization's main focus was on core activities reflected in the traditional value chain described by Michael Porter:[1] purchasing, production, marketing, sales, distribution and customer service. Most of the workforce was engaged in operational work, characterized by such standardized and routine activities as order fulfilment, product assembly, maintenance and customer support.

To support this model, organizations were predominantly structured functionally, in such vertical departments as marketing, sales, logistics, procurement, production, customer service and accounting. Staff skills were developed to improve execution of duties. Management information systems and processes were adjusted to reflect this reality. Each department had its own objectives, and the profitability of the company was shown as such.

Senior executives who were raised in this environment defined the organization's strategies, made decisions, allocated scarce resources and prioritized their work according to the traditional operational model, which I describe as the 'run-the-business' dimension.

---

1   The term 'value chain' was used by Michael Porter in his book *Competitive Advantage: Creating and Sustaining Superior Performance* (1985).

In the late 1980s, however, companies started to engage more and more in project-based activities, which is what I call the '*change-the-business*' dimension. By this I mean one-off, temporary activities with a clear purpose that are performed by multidisciplinary personnel who come together only for specific projects. Operational work, which comprises standardized activities performed on a routine basis, is the opposite of project work.

Since then, and as Figure I.1 shows, more and more organizations have been turning from operations work to project work. Amazingly, however, the academic world has failed to identify this trend. Only a handful of companies have fully exploited the benefits of this shift, many without really knowing that this change was taking place. As I will explain later, one of the companies that perfectly understood this change in paradigm and took full advantage of it is Apple, during the second era of Steve Jobs in the late 1990s.

But this trend has enormous consequences for the way companies are managed – it represents a new paradigm. *The change-the-business dimension is completely different from the run-the-business side in almost every single element*: management, processes, tools, skills, structure, governance, control, performance metrics and so forth. *Because neither management gurus nor the academic world have noticed this trend, it has grown in a unique way within each company.* Despite the differences in how the trend is expressed, it always results in significant conflicts between these two business dimensions, which explains why so many projects fail and so many strategies are not executed successfully.

As we will see, dealing with the trend away from operations work (run-the-business) and toward project work (change-the-business) is not easy and often is a zero sum process: *What you add to one dimension you have to subtract*

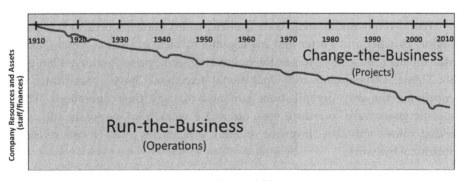

Figure I.1   Ruthless trend – paradigm shift

from another. This calculation has an immediate impact on the side from which something is subtracted, and probably affects the entire business.

To illustrate, some years ago I was working with a company that decided to invest in a strategic project (change-the-business) in the south of Turkey. To find the budget for this project, the chief executive officer (CEO) fired two receptionists (run-the-business) who worked at one of the company's business centres. His thinking was that the value of the project was higher than the added value of the receptionists. This reasoning might seem logical; but in the end, clients visiting the centre were negatively affected and potential sales were lost, thus affecting the core activities of the business. The international expansion project was delivered one year later than promised, with expenses that were three times over budget bringing the company close to bankruptcy. Deciding where to focus companies' scarce resources is one of top management's most important challenges.

Explanations for the Shift toward a Project-Focused Organizational Culture

The following are some of the main explanations for the new paradigm and the trend toward a project-focused environment. I will discuss this trend further in Chapter 1.

REDUCTION/IMPROVEMENTS IN OPERATIONS (RUN-THE-BUSINESS)

Some of the most significant management theories of the past 100 years have focused mainly on increasing efficiency and optimizing the way organizations run and manage their operations (run-the-business).

World-renowned strategists and business management gurus such as Ford, Taylor, Drucker and Porter and management practices such as Total Quality Management, Business Process Reengineering, Enterprise Resource Planning, Six Sigma, Outsourcing and Operational Excellence have concentrated on improving the way organizations run and manage their operations. Their specific goals were to reduce cost, automate work, remove waste and non-added-value activities, improve overall efficiencies and, most recently, outsource the work.

Surprisingly, none of their methods were aimed at executing strategy or improving the way projects were selected and managed in organizations, despite the fact that implementing any of these theories became a large project in itself. Even more surprisingly, none of the management gurus mentioned above discuss projects in any of their theories, or the fact that in order to execute a company strategy you need to have good project management practices and to be focused.

THE CHALLENGES OF IMPROVING PROJECTS (CHANGE-THE-BUSINESS)

Improving operations is easier than improving projects. Often, operational processes can be mapped, analysed and finally improved by automating or simply removing the inefficient parts. This is not possible with projects: mapping them is very complex, and they are very difficult to improve as most of the time they are one-off.

INCREASE IN PROJECTS

The way in which companies create most of their future value is by investing in new technologies, creating new products, opening new markets, reducing costs, increasing productivity and acquiring new businesses. All of these strategic initiatives translate into projects that need to be successfully implemented in order to create value and reach the strategic goals.

Today's market is extremely competitive. Companies need to launch new products quickly, and product lifecycle has been reduced significantly over the last decades. That means that in order to stay in business organizations are required not only to innovate new value-added products but also to reduce time to market. In addition, the fast-changing environment requires that companies become more agile to cope with and react to constant change.

Despite the increasing importance of projects, there is very little literature that addresses the problem from a CEO's or chief finance officer's (CFO's) perspective. The majority of books on project and project portfolio management are directed toward project managers. Yet, the people ultimately in charge of projects are the senior executives (i.e., the 'C-suite' – personnel with the word 'chief' in their job title).

Some of my awareness comes from global surveys I carried out in 2004 and 2006. The surveys were completed by over 400 companies across 30 countries and the results provided me with relevant insights on – and confirmed my views about – the current state of strategy execution and project management.

THE IMPORTANCE OF BEING FOCUSED

My research showed that although very few companies succeed in implementing their strategies, there are a few whose strategy execution is successful. What differentiated these successful companies was that they had a great leaders and high maturity levels in the key elements of their organization.

To my surprise, some of these successful organizations were not just reaching but were also exceeding their strategic objectives. While their formula included great leadership and maturity, what made all the difference in their ability to exceed their expectations was the fact that they were highly FOCUSED.

What I realized is that in today's world *most companies and many employees are highly unfocused*. As a result, top management has difficulty setting a clear strategy and communicating a ranked list of priorities; and most staff members end up deciding on their own where to concentrate their efforts: most likely on easy and irrelevant tasks. This lack of focus results in much wasted money and resources, the inability to execute the strategy, project failures and unhappy and uncommitted employees. *Successful individuals are highly focused, and the same applies to organizations*. In fact, every business is focused when it is just starting up but only those companies that manage to *stay* focused will likely succeed and remain in business.

The best example of a focused organization is Apple under the leadership of Steve Jobs, particularly when he returned in 1997 to turn the company around. In Chapter 4 I will describe how Steve Jobs converted Apple from a highly unfocused company on the verge of bankruptcy into a highly focused and one of the most valuable organization's in the world.

The FOCUSED Organization

FOCUSED can be thought of as an acronym:

- **F – Fewer projects**,[2] rather than many. A focused organization that is able to effectively select and prioritize its projects and invest in just a few good initiatives clearly outperforms organizations that

---

2   Although the acronym emphasizes on fewer projects, a focused organization has fewer products and services as well.

take on too many projects and products. Some of the greatest business leaders, such as Steve Jobs, rightly agree that saying 'no' is one of the most difficult tasks of a leader. Nevertheless, the leaders of any organization that wants to become focused must learn to say 'no' to many initiatives. Subsequently, the focus organization, starting with its CEO, is relentless in executing the prioritized initiatives while filtering out all other distractions.

- **O – Organized staff**. A focused enterprise is made up of the very best professionals and only the best survive. Staff are organized in such a way that all personnel know what is expected of them and how their work contributes to the achievement of strategy. They do not waste time on activities that are not part of their core skill set; rather, they focus on their key strengths and exploit the core competencies of the company. In addition, the key initiatives are managed by the best people.

- **C – Competitive mindset**. The focused company competes with the outside world, externally rather than internally, using innovation and excellence as its main differentiation. Internal competition is minimized because all the organization's effort is concentrated on doing what it does best in order to beat the competition.

- **U – Urgency**. In business, time flies – even more so with the current level of globalization. Organizations need to launch their initiatives quickly. The time-to-market for new products must become shorter and shorter. Creating a sense of 'urgency' is a competitive advantage and is one of the best ways to focus your staff and get their highest performance. The CEO of the focused organization is aware of this fact and knows how to build a sense of urgency whenever things become too complacent.

- **S – Strategic alignment**. In a focused organization all the staff are aware of the strategic objectives of the company and how they will be achieved. Every initiative is linked to a strategic objective. Any project that is not so linked is immediately cancelled (and this book explains how to identify these projects and how to stop them). All departments work in an integrated manner towards achieving those objectives, removing any room for a creation of silos.

- **E – Excellence.** A focused organization is a place where imagination is nurtured, applied and executed while ensuring excellence in all that it does. Employees understand the importance of quality and continuous improvement. They also know that there is no compromise on quality and that they should strive towards perfection, which stretches staff beyond their limits. With this approach there is little room for internal politics.

- **D – Discipline.** Companies today need discipline in order to execute their strategy and their key initiatives; without it, consistent performance becomes very difficult. Of course, there is a need for creativity and flexibility as well. The challenge for the CEO and the company's entire management team is to find the right balance between discipline and creativity/flexibility.

An organization has to go through a large transformation project to reach the status of FOCUSED. To achieve this status very quickly, I propose and explain in detail an accelerated transformation approach that will significantly increase a company's maturity. Reaching the highest maturity levels can take up to five years using traditional maturity models, while with the accelerated transformation method maturity can be reached in 12 months and can provide tangible benefits.

The Focused Organization framework is composed of Six Pillars which the book will help an organization assess and improve:

1. Leaderships and culture.

2. People and skills.

3. Organization and governance.

4. Processes and methods.

5. Systems and tools.

6. Performance management.

The benefits of becoming a focused organization are significant, the most important being:

- **Achievement of strategic goals**. Everybody in the focused organization – from the CEO to the accounts payable employee – knows the direction in which the organization is going; which two to three initiatives are the most important; and the business case for these few critical initiatives. All employees are extremely committed to helping the organization become the best.

- **Greater agility and responsiveness to market changes**. Identifying an optimal balance between the run-the-business and the change-the-business dimensions will bring plenty of benefits to the organization. The result is that one plus one will make three. The organization will become agile and more responsive to market changes and competition. Eventually, the organization can become a trendsetter and market leader.

- **Happy and fully engaged employees**. Focus brings happiness to staff members: they know how to contribute to the company's success; they are proud to belong to it; and they are ready to work harder. The fact that the company will be focused will create less internal tension and more harmony, and work will change from stressful and pressured to positive and rewarding. A healthy and competitive spirit will develop throughout the organization.

- **Positive financial results**. This is probably the most important benefit of becoming a focused organization, since organizations need to have good financial results to survive and to please their shareholders. The focused organization reduces costs by cancelling those projects that are not relevant – a step that can result in huge savings. In addition, the focused organization chooses only those initiatives that will bring significant added value to the group.

- **High performance**. In a focused organization, everybody strives for excellence, and staff are pushed and stretched to do things they have never dreamed possible. Project teams are clearly identified with project objectives/goals and are willing to work hard because they enjoy what they are doing.

- **A culture of getting things done**. Today, many organizations love to discuss new business initiatives, but they stop at the discussion stage. A focused organization selects just a few initiatives and gets them done.

The Book's Structure

The Focused Organization is divided into two major parts. The first part will reveal the alarming fact that although the number of projects in both private and public organizations has increased every year since the middle of the twentieth century, project management as a discipline has not been a priority either for business leaders or the academic community. I will explain why this has happened and the multiple ways in which corporations around the world have suffered the consequences of failing to successfully implement their strategies and projects.

The second part of the book will discuss the characteristics that comprise a focused organization; describe the six pillars within which a focused organization has built its levels of maturity; provide examples of focused organizations that outperform the rest; and explain in practical steps how all enterprises can become focused.

My goal is for this book to be easy to read and, more importantly, easier to implement within your organization. It has practical examples and simple descriptions so that companies can use it right away. It also addresses some points that can easily be expanded upon or deepened by consulting the references.

However, becoming a focused organization involves a radical change in the way businesses are organized and the way they select and manage projects – in fact, the creation of a new culture – and the process will not be easy. Implementing my suggestions will depend in large part on how involved the CEO is in championing the change.

At times, a company implementing these changes will wonder whether it has made the right decision and whether it is going in the right direction. These doubts are a normal part of implementing such a transformational change. It will also take some time to get to the highest level of maturity, but I offer a fast-track approach that will provide most benefits after less than 12 months' work.

I am confident that you will enjoy reading this book – but even more the practice involved in becoming focused.

PART I

*Why Most Companies
Only Partially Achieve
Their Strategies*

Organizational Evolution and the Challenges of Strategy Execution

Organizational evolution over the last 100 years has involved major changes, for example, the move from an industrial economy to an information society and the mass use of personal computers (PCs) and the Internet.

Although these changes have resulted in improvements to organizations' operations, a significant gap exists between companies' strategic plans and the

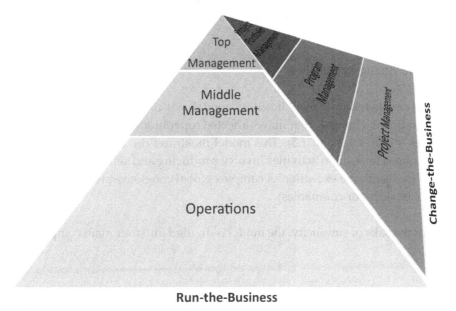

Run-the-Business

Figure 1.1   New paradigm

execution of those plans. The fact is that while companies are running more and more projects, they lack a basic understanding of how to link them with their overall strategy.

This chapter describes a new paradigm, a totally different way of looking at a company's activities: *run-the-business vs change-the-business* – the link between strategy planning, strategy execution and project management. It also discusses why despite the ways in which organizations have evolved, some of their fundamental aspects have not changed.

A simple model (Figure 1.1) illustrates a new way of looking at an organization's activities, which will help explain the current split between operations and projects as well as the challenge of linking strategy planning with strategy execution.

The Composition of a Business

OPERATIONS – ACTIVITIES THAT RUN-THE-BUSINESS

The core element of most organizations is their operations, which include all the activities involved in running the business. If an organization's revenues are derived primarily from its products, its fundamental activities are supply, design, production, distribution, marketing and sales. This concept is reflected in Porter's value chain.[1]

Updated Business Model

I have developed my own business model which takes into account the organizational changes that have affected operations during the last few decades (Figures 1.2 and 1.3). This model illustrates the composition of most companies whose main activities involve producing and selling products and/ or services (with the exception of complex global conglomerates with multiple lines of business or companies).

For the sake of simplicity, the model is divided into four main components:

---

1   The term 'value chain' was used by Michael Porter in his book *Competitive Advantage: Creating and Sustaining Superior Performance* (1985).

Composition of a business that produces and sells goods

Run-the-Business

Figure 1.2   Products value chain

Composition of a business that sells services

Run-the-Business

Figure 1.3   Services value chain

1.   **Shareholders**. Shareholders are the organization's owners. In large and quoted companies shareholders generally comprise big investors, banks, investment funds and other companies. These owners often sit on the board, which decides the composition of the top management and follows up the performance of the company.

2.   **Top management**. Top management is the branch of an organization that both sets and is responsible for defining and executing the company's strategy. This group also oversees the company's day-to-day operations.

3.   **Core activities**. Core activities define the essence of the organization. Their output is the products that are sold to customers and which bring in the revenues that enable the company to continue to operate.

4.   **Support activities**. Support activities, which are now often referred to as 'functions,' aid the company's core processes. In addition, some of the support activities provide information that helps top management make decisions. Finance and accounting, which are clear examples of support functions, control the financial aspects of the business and provide top management with regular updates on performance. Other support functions are information technology (IT) or human resources (HR), which deals with the people-related side of the business.

Some additional information to consider with this model is outlined below:

- These four components need to interact with each other; therefore reaching harmony and having common objectives is important for the stability and future development of the business.

- A business can be profitable if the cost of both core and support activities is less than the price the end customers pay for its products or services.

- The link between activities, including information flow as well as systems and processes for performing activities, is crucial to an organization's success and profitability.

- Most companies excel at one or two of their core activities, which is what differentiates them from the competition. These areas can also be referred to as value drivers or core competencies.

- Many companies do not perform all of their core activities – for example product design, production of components, final assembly and delivery to the end user – by themselves. Some of these core activities are outsourced or involve the purchase of products from other companies. Some of the support activities can also be outsourced, for example, information technology (IT) infrastructure maintenance.

Activities That Comprise the Operations/Run-the-Business Dimension

Operations are not only about managing production activities or plants, but also include the daily activities required to run the business, such as logistics, procurement, finance, sales, customer service, marketing, IT, payroll and so forth. These components involve most of the employees and their worksites; are where management focuses most of their time and attention; and are ultimately the source of the company's day-to-day revenue. Without operations, there is no business.

Increasing a company's growth and profitability purely through operational changes is limited to a few strategic decisions:

- Raising the price of products or services.

- Boosting sales by reducing prices.

- Boosting sales by producing more products or services.

Growing the business and boosting its profitability depends heavily on initiating and successfully completing projects.

The Evolution of Operations

Prior to the adoption of PCs during the 1970s and the 1980s, business operations were tied to plant and production activities. With the move from the industrial age to the service age and then the information age, operations' core focus shifted from production to services to information technology; and the factories of the past have been replaced by IT departments. As will be discussed in detail later, this shift has exponentially increased the number of projects.

Both in the industrial age, with its heavy production, and in the information age, with its dependence on the output of large IT departments, operations consume most of a company's resources in terms of both capacity (workforce) and money (budgets, costs). They also bring in the revenues for the funding of projects.

Examples of Companies' Heavy Operational Focus

Despite all the changes in the business world in the last few decades, most of a company's key elements are still based on this operations model. Some of the most

Table 1.1   Examples of the current strong focus on operations

Elements	Operations Evidence
1. Culture & Leadership	Today, the culture of the company is very much focused on running-the-business/operations. Top management's main priority is to deliver short term results, monthly or quarterly. Most companies lack an execution culture.
2. People & Skills	The majority of the people working in today's organizations are busy working in operations. Career paths are defined for staff working in running-the-business. For example, marketing, sales, and finance staff have more chances of climbing the corporate ladder than staff working in projects. Finally, rewards, yearly bonuses, are pretty much linked to the results of running-the-business. Companies don't have a defined way to reward people delivering successful projects.
3. Organization & Governance	Businesses' organizational charts still strongly reflect their operations and the run-the-business activities. Each of the core and supporting activities is represented in the form of a department, with the responsibilities, resources, and budgets managed by the respective department heads.
4. Processes & Methods	In order to make operations more efficient and less costly, businesses have documented and standardized all of their core and supporting activities. Most of the quality standards, like ISO 9000, focus on standardizing operations. Large companies, in particular, have a strong need for standardization. Another clear example is the accounting rules and the budgeting cycle, which are solely oriented to cover the run-the-business/operations dimension.
5. Systems & Tools	Most of the important systems have been implemented to manage and to monitor run-the-business/operations, in particular the core activities. For example, the main goal of the Enterprise Resource Planning (ERP) systems, which every business now has in place, is to automate sourcing, production, distribution, and finance.
6. Performance Management	Today most of the top management performance monitoring models and applications solely cover the run-the-business/operations dimensions. Reporting is mainly done on the progress and the outcome of the execution of the operations.

evident examples are explained in Table 1.1, and Chapter 2 will discuss the impact of this heavy operational focus on a company's ability to execute its strategy.

PROJECTS: TASKS THAT CHANGE-THE-BUSINESS

The contrasting dimension to a company's operations (run-the-business) is its projects, which are defined as the activities that change-the-business.

Differences Between Projects and Operations

Projects differ from operations in the following ways:

- Projects are one-off investments designed to achieve predetermined objectives, whereas operations are a business's day-to-day activities, with similar objectives every year (with some marginal improvements).

- Projects are restricted in terms of time and budget and are staffed by temporary team members. On the other hand, operations are repetitive, can be more easily automated, operate according to a yearly budget and are staffed by full-time team members.

- Projects need different types of resources from operations. Project leaders need to work transversely to bring different views together and thus require diplomacy and negotiation skills. They also need to be good at managing uncertainty because large strategic projects are not predictable from one week to another.

After a project is completed, the end product/deliverable is often transferred to the operations side of the business, where the anticipated benefits (i.e., the business case for the project) must be achieved successfully. As an example, consider a technology company that decides to run a project to develop a new digital tablet. The estimated cost of the project is €15 million, with expected revenues in the order of €100 million. Once the tablet has been produced, the organization's operations side will take over – with the marketing team launching the product and the sales team selling the tablet and working to achieve the target revenues of €100 million.

Common Projects and Their Strategic Ranking

The most common types of projects and their strategic ranking[2] are illustrated in Table 1.2 on the following page. As the table shows, the most strategic projects have a strong external focus, with a goal that is *revenue and profitability growth* related, while the least strategic projects are internally focused, with a goal that often involves *productivity improvements*, either via cost reduction or increase in asset performance. So, very simplistically, when a company launches a new project one of its main objectives must be to increase growth or improve productivity and performance. The more strategic projects (growth related) are usually sponsored by the business and corporate departments, while the less strategic (productivity related) are launched by the support functions (Figure 1.4).

Chief executive officers (CEOs) and senior management prefer the more strategic initiatives because they produce the highest returns and the greatest benefits. However, such initiatives are usually riskier, more costly and produce benefits that require time to harvest.

---

2   Another good ranking of strategic projects is the FD – Corporate Strategy Study conducted in May 2009, which included 230 interviews with 90 chief executive officers (CEOs).

Table 1.2   Most common types of projects, ranked by strategic importance

	TYPES OF PROJECTS/ STRATEGIC INITIATIVES	STRATEGIC RANKING	TYPE OF INITIATIVE	RISK FACTOR	RETURN ON INVESTMENT	SUCCESS RATE	PAYBACK PERIOD
Most Strategic	Mergers and Acquisitions	AAA	Growth	High	500%	30%	12–36 months
	International Expansion	AAA	Growth	Depending on country	300%	10%–80%	12–24 months
	Innovation - New Products	AAA	Growth	High	200%	10%–30%	6–12 months
	Initial Public Offering	AAA	Growth	Low	150%	90%	6 months
	Rebranding	AA	Growth	Medium	100%	60%	6 months
	Business Transformation	AA	Productivity	High	40%–50%	40%	12–24 months
	Outsourcing	AA	Productivity	Medium	20%–50%	70%	6–24 months
	Internal Reorganization	A	Productivity	Medium	10%	50%	6–12 months
	Downsizing	A	Productivity	Medium	10%–30%	70%	6–12 months
Least Strategic	System Implementation Process Automation	A	Productivity	High	10%–30%	40%	12–36 months

EXTERNAL   INTERNAL

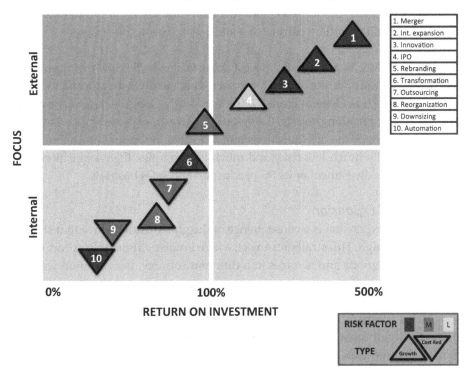

Figure 1.4   Types of projects

Companies must also carry out projects that are *mandatory*, meaning that any changes or adaptations are required by either external regulation (like Basel III in the banking industry) or technical imperatives (upgrades to a new system because the previous one is no longer supported). Finally, companies need to carry out *smaller projects* (which may also be called maintenance projects) that are needed to keep the operations running.

Besides the operational projects, a company needs to have a good overview of the *pipeline of potential new ideas or investment opportunities* and of the value they might bring to the business. Management usually decides to invest in a few ideas, but it is also very important to keep some in the pipeline. Monitoring and managing ideas helps management react quickly to changes in the market, either in a defensive way or a proactive way.

Mergers and Acquisitions (M&A)
Thompson Financial reported that in 2005 the worldwide M&A deal volume was $2.7 trillion. M&A projects include the merger of two companies, the

acquisition of a company or the sale (carve-out) of a business. Thus, M&As are the most strategic type of project, and probably the fastest way of generating significant profits (both by cutting cost and by increasing revenues).

However, M&As are also the riskiest projects. It is well know that more than half of mergers fail or do not deliver the expected benefits.[3] On the other hand, some companies – such as General Electric or more recently Google – have made an art of executing acquisition projects. Carve-outs or divestments are similar strategic initiatives, the opposite of acquisitions but important in shaping future business. They are usually much less risky and much less complex than acquisitions: for example, IBM's divestment of its PC production and sales business.

International Expansion

International expansion is a consequence of the globalization wave that started many decades ago. This strategic project, which involves a business's production and/or sale of goods and services in a different country, is a common way for companies to generate growth.

Once a company has reached a certain level of maturity and market share domestically, it must find additional areas in which to grow. Entering a new market is a complex project because of differences in culture, legislation and other unknowns. In addition, companies that expand internationally need to take into account currency fluctuations, which sometimes can make the difference between a deal worth doing and a deal that would be a disaster.

The main expansion areas this decade are the emerging markets of Brazil, Russia, India and China (BRIC countries) – particularly China, which is considered to be the new El Dorado. However, thus far there have been many failures in attempts to expand into China. To mitigate the risks, companies often form joint ventures with local companies already established in that market.

Innovation – New Product Introduction[4]

Companies need to innovate constantly to stay alive. New product development projects are necessary to maintain market share because demand for most

---

3   Various studies have shown that mergers have failure rates of more than 50 per cent. One recent study found that 83 per cent of all mergers fail to create value, and that half actually destroy value. See Robert W. Holthausen, The Nomura Securities Company Professor at the Wharton School, University of Pennsylvania at http://accounting.wharton.upenn.edu/people/faculty.cfm?id=408.

4   Innovation also applies for new service introduction for businesses that operate in the service industry.

brands, products and even services tends to decline over time. New product development projects are also necessary in order to respond to the competition as well as to new technologies and changing market conditions.

There are two parallel paths involved in new product development: one involves idea generation, product design and detail engineering; the other involves market research and marketing analysis. The actual project usually takes place during the first stage. Market research and marketing analysis are usually part of running-the-business activities.

The ultimate goal of innovation projects is to increase market share and revenues. The benefits are often estimated in terms of increase in market share, sales and profitability. The expected return on investment should be at least 10 per cent. Most innovation projects fail. However, most companies still dedicate a large portion of their resources to introducing new products.

Initial Public Offering (IPO)

When a company reaches a certain stage in its growth, it might decide to go public with an initial public offering. The main goal here is to quickly raise capital for further business expansion and growth (i.e., additional strategic projects). Deciding to go public and sell part of the available stock is a strategic decision – and a very intensive one – that absorbs lots of management attention (i.e., the CEO and/or chief finance officer (CFO) are often away for weeks on promotional roadshows).

Unlike other strategic projects, most IPOs are successful – at least at first. This can be explained by the huge amount of top management attention that such projects receive; their relatively minimal impact on day-to-day business operations; and the full-time dedication of a small team. In addition, IPOs have the support of investment bankers, consultants and lawyers who are very familiar with these types of projects.

A major benefit of IPOs is fast access to public capital, at least in the short term. The riskier part of IPOs comes with time: when the company needs to keep up with the fast pace of quarterly reporting; to show regular profitability; and to deal with the increase in regulatory scrutiny. The biggest risk is stock market volatility, which can result in drops in share price – and in the associated dissatisfied shareholders.

Rebranding

Rebranding is not a very common project, but it is considered highly strategic. This project might involve radical changes to the company's name, image, logo, marketing strategy and advertising themes. These changes are aimed at repositioning the company's brand, sometimes in an attempt to distance itself from certain negative connotations from the past (e.g., Chapter 11 bankruptcy in the USA) or to move the brand to a different segment in the market. The objective is to communicate a new message. Rebranding can also be applied to new products, mature products or even products still in development. Good examples of rebranding are those completed by Apple or BP, who changed their logos some years ago.

Although rebranding affects many aspects of an organization, this type of project is not very complex and involves simply making the right choices for the company's new image. A rebranding project's ultimate purpose is to increase revenues and market share, but its exact return on investment is difficult to assess.

Business Transformation
Business transformation is a strategic change project that aims to more closely align a company's people, processes and systems initiatives with its business strategy and vision. This type of project involves changing from one 'look' to another or from one culture to another, which in turn helps develop and support new business strategies. It can also include the development of new manufacturing processes and of new facilities and infrastructure for the business.

Transformation and change are critical issues for most organizations. If visible change has not taken place (both inside and out) then the change project is not transformational. Research shows that the failure rates of change projects are around 70 per cent, with such failure often signaling the end of a business.

Business transformation can be triggered by internal or external factors. Internal factors may be driven by the need to continually improve performance. External factors may be driven by competitors, changing markets and regulations. For instance, the business models of Indian software giants such as Infosys, TCS and Wipro have all undergone many successful transformations in the decades they have been in existence.

The benefits of transformation projects are difficult to quantify in monetary terms, but good transformations make companies more successful overall.

Outsourcing
Outsourcing projects are usually related to technology initiatives – such as handing over IT infrastructure maintenance to a third party – but they can

also relate to non-technical services such as contracting out telephone-based customer service departments, design, marketing or even accounting services.

Although the primary objective of an outsourcing project is often cost reduction, many businesses fail to realize any cost benefits. One of Gartner Research's 2007 predictions was that 80 per cent of organizations that outsource customer service projects with the primary goal of cutting costs would fail in that attempt.[5] The reasoning behind this statistic is the considerable staff attrition rate at outsourcing companies, sometimes as high as 80–100 per cent. Combine this added cost from attrition with the hidden costs of client loss due to increased frustration and it is clear that an outsourcing engagement, if not carefully monitored, can easily fail.

The usual benefits of an outsourcing project can be a 5–15 per cent reduction in the cost of running the outsourced service, which is much lower than what outsourcing service providers promise (sometimes as much as 50 per cent). The issue in recent years, with the downturn in the economy, is that companies are so desperate to save money that they rush through the due diligence process.

Internal Reorganization

As Alfred Chandler stated, 'structure follows strategy.'[6] Therefore, structures are usually reorganized when there are strategic changes – which often happen when a new CEO arrives. There are many types of reorganization projects: merger of companies and organizations, decentralization of business units, centralization and so forth. Today, one of the most common reorganization projects is the relocation of some part of the business to Asia, and in particular to China. The reasoning behind this type of project is that being closer to the largest market in the world will help companies penetrate the Chinese market.

The benefits of reorganization projects are difficult to quantify in monetary terms. The main benefits are qualitative at first. By changing the structure of an organization, management expects to trigger additional growth for the business by improving productivity. Another objective of reorganization projects can be to reduce costs (centralization vs decentralization).

All too often, reorganization projects end in the continuation of existing practices under a new name or, at worst, result in the company's deterioration.

---

5   See http://www.gartner.com/technology/research.jsp.
6   A.D. Chandler Jr (1962), *Strategy and Structure: Chapters in the History of the American Industrial Enterprise*, 14.

Often, the effort required to complete these projects is underestimated. Possible reasons for this are that people, processes and systems are assumed to be more flexible than they actually are. Often the reorganization takes longer to implement than foreseen, making employees feel insecure or frustrated. Consequently employees are discouraged, become less committed and some of the best employees may eventually leave the company.

Downsizing

With today's economic instability, most businesses see cost-cutting – in particular, downsizing – as a fast way of securing growth and achieving efficiencies, despite the fact that past research shows that downsizing does not guarantee performance returns. For example, in 2010 the Royal Bank of Scotland (RBS) laid off more than 2,500 employees.

Downsizing projects are often difficult to manage. Management mistakes in handling the laying-off process can lead to employee distrust, reduced employee commitment and morale, and an increase in voluntary turnover. In the short term, the benefits are clear and have a direct effect on the company's bottom line. However, it is not clear that the benefits remain in the mid to long term.

System Implementation/Process Automation

System implementation to automate production, operational and support processes is one of the principal areas that companies invested in during the 1980s. Since then, most companies have installed a number of the following programs: ERP software, sales force automation, customer relationship management, help desk, sales quotation and lead tracking. Implementing any new information system, or updating a current system, is a drain on a company's most valuable resources – time and people, for example.

System implementation projects are known for often being delivered late and with large budget overruns. The promised benefits are often not fully met. SAP implementations, for example, have been famous for their complexity.

How Projects Affect an Organization

If we look at how projects impact our theoretical business model, we can see that they do not follow a regular pattern (Figure 1.5). Most strategic projects – for example, large acquisitions – have an impact on the entire organization, are highly complex undertakings and require a fully dedicated team, the participation of large numbers of staff members and high levels

Impacts of projects on an organization

Figure 1.5   **Projects go in all directions**

of management. The same is true for expansions into new markets and new product development. On the other hand, productivity improvement projects often address one specific area of the business, for instance, HR's implementation of a new payroll system.

The least strategic projects of all, the so-called 'maintenance' projects, also consume lots – sometimes as much as 10–20 per cent – of change-the-business resources. To avoid this significant expenditure and the possibility of running hundreds of these smaller initiatives, a company must have clear policies on what constitutes a project.

Companies today have trouble prioritizing projects as well as cancelling the ones that are unsuccessful. When there are too many highly strategic projects, the company will be stretched thin, there will be little time to think and some people will become burned out. The consequence will be that most of the strategic initiatives will fail or not deliver the expected return. In addition, a company that is running too many projects will have trouble prioritizing them and consequently may waste money and gain a low return on investment.

Allocation of Financial and Staff Resources

Companies do not have the financial or staff resources to invest in an unlimited number of new initiatives. In principle, management is faced with the challenge of prioritizing new projects and choosing which ones to implement. I say 'in principle' because, as will be discussed later, senior management is often unable to handle this challenge. During the past decade, many companies have fallen

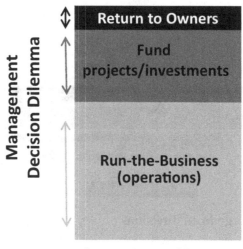

Figure 1.6   Challenge of allocating company assets and resources

into the trap of accepting new ideas and implementing far more new projects than they could possibly handle – in my opinion for either of two reasons:

- Management is not used to saying 'no' and accepts any idea that has a decent business case because it might be successful.

- Management is not used to saying 'stop,' which results in the failure to cancel projects once they have begun.

However, with the growth in the number and range of potential projects – coupled with a need for increased effectiveness in a highly competitive world and the recent global financial and economic crisis – this has changed. Management has been forced to be much more selective about their investments and their overall spending. They are now compelled to prioritize projects and to cancel the unsuccessful ones. As can be seen in Figure 1.6, a company has three different ways of allocating its assets, staff resources and financial capacity: run-the-business operations; fund projects/investments; return dividends to owners.

1.   **Run-the-business/operations**. Financing operations is critical to any business. Traditionally, almost all of a business's staff resources and financial capacity have gone into running its core and supporting activities. Investing money in operations, as opposed to

projects, is less risky and provides a much faster return. The short-term returns from operations are what keep the business alive.

2.   **Fund projects/investments**. In the short term, funding projects is less critical than funding operations. There are always more project ideas than there is available financial and staff capacity. Besides, projects are riskier endeavours and are not always successful. However, projects are the only way a company can generate much higher returns and differentiate itself from the competition. If a company's strategy is to grow, improve and be more efficient – which is the case for all profit-generating businesses – then projects are critical.

3.   **Return dividends to owners**. The third way in which a company can allocate its resources and financial capacity is to return part of its profits and excess capacity to the owners. Quoted companies usually distribute dividends once a year – and shareholders expect this. Occasionally, companies with surplus cash may decide to return more money to the owners, but this is an exception.

The Challenge of Funding Strategic Projects

One of the main challenges for top management is to decide how to allocate the company's limited finances. A shortage of funds can be overcome by borrowing from banks, from the owners or from other investors. In the past, any company with an interesting idea, a solid business case and a willingness to take the risk for that idea would usually secure funding.

Today, however, due to the global financial crisis, finding external funding is much more difficult and most strategic projects must be financed with excess internal capacity. For those companies that have managed to survive the crisis and come out stronger, this is an excellent time to invest in such strategic projects as acquisitions or new products. However, many of these cash-rich companies are that way precisely because they did not risk making such investments. These companies are usually highly skilled at cost control/awareness but at the expense of growing and strengthening their entrepreneurial skills.

An interesting dichotomy is that most of those businesses that have cash do not know in which strategic projects to invest, while those businesses that want to invest in projects do not have the necessary cash. This dichotomy is much evident in the financial sector, where the institutions and banks that failed had invested in high-risk strategic projects, and those that survived had not taken many risks.

The Issue of Staffing Strategic Projects

In my opinion, the other big issue involves allocating limited staff resources. For example, the staff in a telecom company are dedicated primarily to operational activities, both core and support. They are busy running the business, leaving very limited personnel – possibly only ten per cent of the total workforce – fully dedicated to projects.[7]

More important, the number of operational staff working part-time on projects has been increasing every year. These employees have to balance their day-to-day responsibilities with the unpredictability of project work; and, as I will explain later, this dual pressure has a big impact on the projects' success.

The big consulting firms have benefited enormously from the fact that companies lack sufficient resources to carry out their project activity. These firms have resources readily available, they are experienced and they can be dedicated full-time to projects. This is why so many companies prefer, or are forced, to use consultants if they want to execute some of their strategic projects. The problem with this approach is that companies become dependent on consultants to do a significant part of their strategic work, which are more expensive than own resources, and they often are not able to keep knowledge in-house.

Management often prefers to invest excess money in new strategic projects, believing that a successful outcome will lead to a higher return. This has an impact on resources too. As mentioned previously, too many initiatives – particularly too many strategic ones – create a lack of focus, which leads to a failure in the execution of the strategy and sometimes even to bankruptcy.

One example of this is the Belgian bank Fortis, which in 2006 and 2007 invested in several high-return but high-risk initiatives in a race to achieve double-digit growth every quarter. At the same time that Fortis bought a small division of highly specialized financial engineers in the United States to build

---

7   This is a rough estimate, with the percentage depending on the industry, the maturity of the market and the phase of the business. Within a company, this percentage also varies between departments.

and sell collateralized debt obligations (CDOs), top management decided to engage in the largest ever takeover in the financial sector. Fortis formed part of a consortium of three, with RBS and Banco Santander. On 23 April 2007, the consortium made an offer of €72 billion – €5 billion higher than the offer by Barclays, the other contender. The result was too many strategic initiatives, too much risk and a lack of focus, which was made even worse by the global financial crisis. Eighteen months after the acquisition, Fortis was on the verge of bankruptcy. The Belgian government intervened, and Fortis was partially nationalized on 28 September 2008. As we can see, and not only in Fortis's case, the race for growth can push companies to invest in more strategic initiatives than they can handle.

The Link between Strategic Planning and Strategy Execution

DEFINITION OF STRATEGY

'Strategy' is a word of military origin, referring to a plan of action designed to achieve particular goals. In this usage, a strategy is distinct from a tactic – the latter being concerned with the execution of a specific initiative – and instead focuses on how different initiatives are linked to accomplish certain objectives.

COMPONENTS OF A WELL-DEFINED STRATEGIC PLAN

A well-defined strategic plan shows:

1. Vision – where the company wants to be in the long term (5–10 years). This component should not be simply a list of objectives, such as 10 per cent growth in market share; it must be a way in which the company wants to differentiate itself.

2. Core competencies and key advantages that set the company apart from the competition.

3. Product(s)/service(s) that the company will produce/sell.

4. Market(s) in which the company will operate.

5. Resources that the company needs in order to be able to operate in the chosen markets.

6.   Shareholders' expectations.

7.   The market environment – external factors (i.e., regulations) that affect the company's ability to compete.

8.   Strategic objectives, which are the targets that the company should achieve (these targets should be quantifiable and linked to the overall vision, but often they are not).

Large organizations usually have two different levels of strategy:

- Business-specific strategies, which define the products/services that the organization will sell in the selected market. Usually, business-specific strategies encompass short- and medium-term decisions.

- Overall strategy for the entire organization, also called corporate strategy, which is usually defined for the long term – including key values of the organization.

To understand how strategy works, let us refer again to our business model. The first part of the strategy focuses on the strengths of the company's operations (run-the-business): value drivers, core competencies, core values, products/ services it will sell and the markets in which it will operate. The second part of the strategic plan is the definition of the company's vision, which is where it wants to be in the mid and long term. This definition will affect how the operations evolve over the time and it is mainly carried out through projects (change-the-business).

RELATIONSHIP BETWEEN STRATEGY EXECUTION AND PROJECTS

Once the strategic plan's components have been established, the next step is to define the targets, or strategic objectives. There are two main types of objectives that should be in a strategic plan:

Operational: Run-the-Business Objectives

Operational objectives are performance, financial and commercial goals that a company seeks to reach within a year, or at most within three years. These targets are needed to make sure the company continues to grow and continues to produce money. Most of a company's efforts are focused on these short-term objectives.

Strategic: Change-the-Business Objectives

Strategic objectives generally involve mid-to long-term goals and, as such, are less tangible and quantifiable than operational objectives. These targets are aimed at transforming the business to significantly increase the company's growth and profitability.

Once the strategic objectives have been fixed, the final step is to *define the programmes that will make the company reach those objectives*. These programmes are primarily linked to the change-the-business objectives and initiatives, which should then be broken down into potential projects which later on should be approved and prioritized.

To better understand this dichotomy between run- and change-the-business objectives, I looked at the strategies of 40 of CNN.com's list of the *Fortune* Global 500 in 2010.[8] I determined that when they are defining their strategies, most companies do not differentiate between operational and strategic objectives. In addition, the objectives are not all measurable. Finally, companies do not specify how they are going to reach those objectives (i.e., in which projects they are going to invest). I am not saying that companies should publicly identify those projects, but they should do so internally.

In fact, by looking into a company's strategic objectives and projects, together with its capabilities to execute those projects, we can get a good idea of whether that company has any chances of achieving its strategic goals. As an illustration, outlined below are the strategic objectives of the top three companies in the world according to the Forbes Global ranking.

1.   **Walmart**[9] (rank 1; revenues in 2010: $408,214 million):

     •   Dominate the retail market wherever Walmart has a presence (run-the-business/operations).

     •   Grow by expansion in the US and internationally (change-the-business/projects).

---

8   See http://edition.cnn.com.
9   See http://walmartstores.com.

- Create widespread name recognition and customer satisfaction with the Walmart brand, and associate the retailer with the reputation of offering the best prices (both run- and change-the business).

- Branch out into new sectors of retailing such as pharmacies, automotive repair and grocery sales (change-the-business/ projects).

2. **Royal Dutch Shell**[10] (rank 2; revenues in 2010: $285,129 million):

- Reinforce position as a leader in the oil and gas industry in order to provide a competitive shareholder return while helping to meet global energy demand in a responsible way. Entering a new period of growth, sharpen up performance and reduce costs (change-the-business/projects).

- In Upstream, explore new oil and gas reserves and develop major projects where the company's technology and know-how add value to the resource holders. Upstream production is expected to reach 3.5 million barrels of oil equivalent per day (mboe/d) in 2012, an increase of 11 per cent from 2009. In addition, the company is assessing over 35 new projects from some 8 billion boe resources, which should underpin Upstream growth to 2020 (change-the-business/projects).

- Downstream continues to focus on profitability, with plans to exit 15 per cent of refining capacity and 35 per cent of retail markets, and growth investment to enhance the quality of manufacturing and marketing portfolios. As new projects come on stream, the company expects cash flow from operations to increase by around 50 per cent from 2009 to 2012 in a $60/barrel (bbl) oil price world, and by over 80 per cent with $80/bbl oil prices (both run- and change-the-business).

3. **Toyota**[11] (rank 5; revenues in 2010: $204,106 million):

---

10 See http://www.shell.com.
11 See http://www.toyota-global.com.

- Increase supply of low CO_2/fuel-efficient vehicles – hybrid (HV) and compact (both run- and change-the-business).

- Improve profitability through cost reduction (change-the-business/projects).

- Expand operations in resource-rich countries and emerging markets – full entry into the Indian and Brazilian markets (change-the-business/projects).

- Accelerate plug-in hybrid and electric vehicle (PHV and EV) development (change-the-business/projects).

What becomes clear when looking at the strategies of these top companies is that in order to reach most of their strategic objectives, they will need to execute *projects*. If Walmart wants to grow by expansion in the US, if Shell wants to find additional oil and gas reserves and if Toyota wants to increase its operations in Brazil, each will need to select, and execute successfully, the right projects.

In addition, by looking at these top 40 companies I could identify those that are more or less focused; those taking more risks; those looking for higher returns; and those that have a more cautious approach and are thus more focused on running their day-to-day activities. I could also see which of them will need a greater project management and strategy execution maturity if they want to reach their objectives. Finally, all of the top 40 companies have strategic projects, even if they are not defined as such.

The Trend Toward More Projects

One important finding of my research is the silent but persistent trend toward more projects that has affected probably every business in the last century.

EXPLANATIONS FOR THE TURN FROM OPERATIONS WORK TO PROJECT WORK

As illustrated by Figure 1.7, since the 1920s (or even earlier) companies have been improving their run-the-business/operations activities as a means of increasing productivity by becoming more efficient and reducing costs. At that time, most companies were mainly producing goods – the service industry

Over the past century, projects have become more and more important

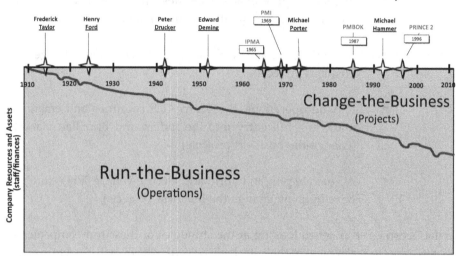

Figure 1.7   Ruthless trend

was not yet strong – and one of their main objectives was to grow. Growth by acquisition was not as popular as it is today, so the growth was mainly organic – by increasing production capacity and by entering new markets. Once the industries became more mature, growth was achieved by increasing efficiencies and reducing costs. The impact of these growth techniques was that the number of projects increased over time.

In addition, an important element that significantly influenced this trend was the fact that almost all the management gurus and their management theories focused on improvements for the run-the-business dimension. As I will explain in Chapter 2, Taylor, Ford, Ansoff, Drucker, Porter and other key influencers' recommendations were focused on improving the operations of the business. On the other hand, all of these operational improvements were carried out as projects. These were often one-off projects,[12] but changing a business involves carrying out a project; there is no other way.

Apart from management gurus' contributions during the past few decades towards improving business operations, several other movements have helped accelerate this trend:

---

12 Modern project management most likely evolved from construction projects after World War II. Henry Gantt developed the Gantt chart in the 1910s. The Critical Path Method (DuPont Corporation) and the PERT Method (Booz Allen Hamilton) were invented in the 1950s. The Project Management Institute was founded in 1969 to define project management standards and develop the profession.

- 1970s – the universalization of the PC at work.

- 1980s – the business process reengineering wave.

- 1990s – enterprise resource planning (ERP) to automate most operations.

- 2000s – the outsourcing of core and supporting operations, together with consolidation of the Internet as a new channel for doing business.

The result of all of these changes is that companies have made their operations extremely efficient, reaching levels where finding additional efficiency improvements is no longer possible. The problem is that this increase in projects has gone almost unnoticed because the focus has always been on running-the-business activities. As we will see, dealing with the trend away from operations work (run-the-business) and toward project work (change-the-business) is not easy – and often is a zero sum process: what you add to one dimension you have to subtract from the other. This calculation has an immediate impact on the side from which something is subtracted, and probably affects the entire business.

THE ECONOMIC EXPLANATION OF THE TREND

Another way of understanding this trend is to look at the evolution of the economy. Governments' and central banks' economic and monetary structures have a direct impact on the number of projects. The amount of money in circulation in the economy, the availability of 'cheap' money (i.e., low interest rates) and the velocity of the money (average frequency with which a unit of money is spent) can be indicators of this trend. The more money there is in the economy, the more companies use it to invest in strategic projects. The lower the interest rates, the more companies borrow to invest in strategic projects. To explain this, I looked at the gross domestic product (GDP) evolution of the past century in the UK,[13] making the following assumptions:

- In recession years (negative GDP), companies reduce their spending on projects.

- In years with no GDP growth, nothing changes.

---

13 Bank of England, GDP evolution from 1900 to 2010.

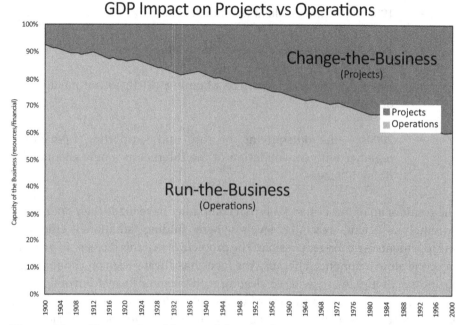

Figure 1.8   **Economic evidence of the trend**

- In years with growth (positive GDP), companies increase their spending on projects.

The impact of these increases or decreases was felt the following year. Figure 1.8 shows the result of my analysis. Astonishingly, the results are very similar to the business trend explained above.

Failure to Link Project Management with Strategy Execution

Despite this increase in projects, project management did not become a recognized profession until the late 1970s and has not yet been recognized as a fundamental method of executing company strategy.

The creation of the Project Management Institute (PMI)[14] in 1969 in Philadelphia can be considered the turning point in the profession – but it still took at least two decades for project management to be seen as an industry best practice. In the UK, project management was not recognized until the 1980s when the government developed the Prince 2 (Projects in Controlled

---

14 See http://www.pmi.org.

Environments)[15] project management methodology for IT projects. Both developments have done a lot for professionalizing project management and developing official certifications for project managers. On the other hand, neither the PMI nor the Prince 2 methodology focused on showing senior executives the value of project management.

The fact that the increase in projects had gone unnoticed for so many years has had a serious impact on businesses in terms of strategy execution. I will explain the consequences of this negligence in detail in Chapter 3.

15 See http://www.ogc.gov.uk/methods_prince_2.asp.

2

Evidence of the Neglect of Project Management

The Origins of Current Views of Project Management

I have spent the last ten years trying to understand why senior executives seem to neither understand project management nor regard it as an important means of strategy execution. While conducting my research, I discovered that most heads of organizations view project management as a highly technical discipline – an area for engineers, information technology (IT) professionals and project managers. Consequently, they:

- Lack a basic understanding of how to link each of their strategic projects with the company's overall strategy.

- Do not devote much time to developing project management competencies in-house.

- Fail to implement a formal project selection process and investment committee to discuss, prioritize and decide on all the new project proposals.

- Lack the means to monitor the success or failure of their strategic projects.

- And therefore do not spend enough time following up the execution of projects.

But why do so many senior executives feel this way? In an attempt to get to the deeper reasons for their views, I sought answers to the following questions:

1.   Do the theories of the most highly regarded business management gurus – those who influence the way businesses are managed (e.g., Taylor, Drucker and Porter) – mention project management and/or the importance of its link with strategy execution?

2.   Have the top business schools, those that train most senior executives and future leaders, been teaching the value of project management and its link with strategy execution?

3.   Do the most prestigious strategic consulting firms advise chief executive officers (CEOs) and other senior executives on the advantages of linking strategy execution with project management?

4.   Is project management regularly discussed in the finest business publications?

Disregard by Business Management Gurus

My rationale for scrutinizing the work of the so-called 'business management gurus' is that they have shaped the way companies do business today. Their theories have promoted big waves of change and improvement for many decades and have become obligatory reading for most business school students.

I looked at business management experts of the twentieth and early twenty-first centuries whom I considered to be the most influential. My aim was to first understand the impact of their theories on business and then to determine whether they discussed project management as a discipline and/or its link to strategy execution.

Frederick Winslow Taylor (20 March 1856–21 March 1915)

SUMMARY OF KEY PREMISES

Considered the father of scientific management, Frederick Winslow Taylor sought to improve industrial efficiency by systematically breaking tasks down into their component elements in an effort to find the single best way to complete them. He is noted for his time-and-motion studies, which involved using a stopwatch to time a worker's sequence of motions, eliminating unnecessary motions and then determining how the task could be performed more efficiently.

Taylor's main theories about how to improve worker productivity were presented in his 1911 publication *The Principles of Scientific Management*:

1.   Replace rule-of-thumb work methods with methods based on a scientific study of the tasks.

2.   Scientifically select, train and develop employees rather than passively leaving them to train themselves.

3.   Provide detailed instruction and supervision of each worker in the performance of his or her specific task.

4.   Divide work nearly equally between managers and workers so that the managers apply scientific management principles to planning the work and the workers actually perform the tasks.

Scientific management was revolutionary because its methods advocated breaking a job down into a sequence of steps that any worker could easily be trained to complete. Prior to this point, jobs were performed by skilled craftsmen who learned their trade through long and expensive apprenticeships.

HOW KEY PREMISES CHANGED BUSINESSES AND INCREASED PROJECTS

During the industrial age, scientific management changed the way companies looked at production. Industrial plants and factories, in particular, launched initiatives to improve production efficiencies. These initiatives can be viewed as projects, since they were time limited and independent of daily operations. In fact, each of the four points in Taylor's principles of scientific management was a project in itself:

•   Scientific study/analysis.

•   Training.

•   Implementation of detailed instructions.

•   Equal allocation of work between workers and managers.

Thus, Taylor's theories, without mentioning the fact, led to a significant increase in organization project activity. But this increase was just temporary; once the improvements in the production processes were made, the companies returned to their operations/run-the-businesses activities.

MENTION OF PROJECT MANAGEMENT AND ITS LINK WITH STRATEGY EXECUTION

Although applying Taylor's theories increased the number of projects undertaken by organizations, these theories did not discuss project management or its value; nor did they link it with strategy execution.

Peter Drucker (19 November 1909–11 November 2005)

SUMMARY OF KEY PREMISES

Peter Drucker's pioneering work helped management theory to become regarded as a serious discipline. He is believed to have either originated or greatly affected almost every aspect of management. In addition, he spent most of his career exploring how humans are organized across all sectors of society. Some of Drucker's major contributions in a career spanning more than six decades are outlined below.

- In the 1940s, Drucker introduced his theories of simplification and decentralization, which recommend that companies avoid producing too many products, hiring employees they do not need, and expanding into sectors with which they are unfamiliar.

- In the 1950s, Drucker discussed his belief that employees are assets and, as such, should be valued. He also shared his view that, rather than simply being a money-making enterprise, a corporation is a community built on trust and respect for its workers.

- Rather than focusing primarily on corporate number-crunching, Drucker's writings explore relationships between people. In particular, he was fascinated by employees who worked with their heads, not their hands, and produced information and ideas. He studied their role within organizations and, in 1959, coined the term 'knowledge workers' to refer to them.

- That same decade, Drucker's seemingly simple idea – that a company's primary responsibility is to serve its customers – was the foundation of a new marketing approach.

- In the 1960s, Drucker argued for the importance of substance over style and for institutionalized practices over trendy leadership policies. He challenged companies to rethink how they executed all of their business processes.

- In the 1970s, Drucker wrote about how knowledge would trump raw material as a modern economy's most critical ingredient.

HOW KEY PREMISES CHANGED BUSINESSES AND INCREASED PROJECTS

Many of Drucker's theories advocated restructuring and thereby improving the way in which managers ran their companies and supervised their employees. Implementing these initiatives was not easy because it required profound changes in management mindset. Consequently, the associated increase in projects was extensive but not immediate. Business leaders took several decades before they put Drucker's theories into action. In addition, companies developed training programmes and changed some human resources (HR) policies to increase knowledge of their workers and business leaders.

Often, the resulting projects lasted for several years and, similar to what happened with Taylor's improvement initiatives, were not seen as projects. During the period when Drucker introduced most of his ideas (1950–1980) companies were not yet familiar with the principles of 'change management,'[1] so the implementation of his improvements encountered much resistance.

MENTION OF PROJECT MANAGEMENT AND ITS LINK WITH STRATEGY EXECUTION

Drucker's theories do not specifically mention project management. However, his idea of companies challenging their way of executing their own business processes does imply a link between strategy execution and project management.

---

1   The concept of 'change management' was introduced by John Kotter in 1996 in his book *Leading Change.*

Igor Ansoff (12 December 1918–14 July 2002)

SUMMARY OF KEY PREMISES

As the pioneer of strategic management, Igor Ansoff developed a unique set of theories based on analyses of his predecessors' work combined with his own insights into the variables that contribute to successful strategies.

Prior to the publication in 1965 of Ansoff's landmark book *Corporate Strategy*, companies lacked guidance on how to plan for the future. Traditionally, they developed a budget and projected it several years into the future but paid little attention to strategic and execution issues. Ansoff stressed in his book that in a business environment characterized by growing competition; an increase in mergers, acquisitions and diversification; and mounting turbulence it was essential to anticipate future challenges and to draw up appropriate strategies to respond to these challenges. Ansoff's research focused primarily on three areas:

1. **The concept of environmental turbulence**. The stable post-war economy was replaced by an atmosphere of rapid and fluctuating change, and Ansoff sought to respond to this by introducing a better framework for strategy formulation.

2. **The contingent strategic success paradigm**, which views strategy development as an ongoing process. Ansoff categorized organizational decisions into four standard types: strategy, policy, programmes and standard operating procedures. The last three, he noted, are developed to resolve recurring problems and do not need to be formulated more than once. Strategy decisions, however, always apply to new situations and must be designed afresh each time.

3. **Real-time strategic issue management**, which is the response to a rapid and unpredicted environmental development. A *strategic issue* is a forthcoming development, either inside or outside of the organization, which is likely to have an important impact on the ability of the enterprise to meet its objectives. An issue may be a welcome issue, an *opportunity to* be grasped in the environment, or an internal *strength* which can be exploited to advantage. Or it can be an unwelcome external *threat,* or an internal *weakness,* which imperils continuing success, even the survival of the enterprise.

Components of Strategy

To establish a link between a corporation's past management approaches and strategic management, Ansoff identified four key strategy components:

- **Product-market scope** – a clear idea of what business or products a company is responsible for.

- **Growth vector** – an exploration of how growth can occur.

- **Competitive advantage** – the organization's strengths that will enable it to compete effectively.

- **Synergy** – the idea that the whole is greater than the sum of the parts. This requires the organization to examine how opportunities fit its core capabilities.

The Ansoff Matrix

In a 1957 *Harvard Business Review* article, Ansoff introduced a marketing tool aimed at helping businesses determine their product and market growth strategies.[2] This tool, the Ansoff matrix, suggests that companies' attempts to grow depend on whether they are marketing new or existing products in new or existing markets. The four strategies given in the matrix include:

1. **Market penetration**, which requires increasing existing product share in existing markets.

2. **Market expansion**, which involves identifying new customers for existing products.

3. **Product expansion**, which entails developing new products for existing customers.

4. **Diversification**, which calls for new products to be produced for new markets.

The matrix describes, in particular, how the element of risk increases the further the strategy moves from known quantities. Thus, product

---

2   H.I. Ansoff, Strategies for diversification, *Harvard Business Review*, 35(5), 113–24.

development and market extension generally involve taking on more risk than would market penetration, which involves existing products and markets. Diversification, entering new markets with new products, carries the greatest risk of all.

HOW KEY PREMISES CHANGED BUSINESSES AND INCREASED PROJECTS

Ansoff's strategic management theories had a twofold impact on the number of projects at most companies. At first, companies formed strategy departments and began to implement Ansoff's teachings through new projects. During this first wave, the primary entities that benefited were consulting companies which used Ansoff's concepts to advise businesses in developing their strategies.

In the 1970s and 1980s, when the establishment of strategic planning departments was very popular, companies significantly increased their projects. One reason for this upsurge was that strategic planning created greater transparency, allowing companies to have a better view of the different initiatives and translating into more projects. However, companies quickly encountered trouble because the strategic planning process did not cover how to execute multiple projects. At this point, the gap between strategy planning and strategy execution widened and increased every year.

MENTION OF PROJECT MANAGEMENT AND ITS LINK WITH STRATEGY EXECUTION

As mentioned above, at first Ansoff's theories increased organizations' projects only slightly. Once the new strategic development offices were created, however, the number of projects exploded. Ansoff does mention the concept of programmes, but he neither expands on it nor explains the link between project management and strategy execution.

Thomas J. Peters (7 November 1942–)

SUMMARY OF KEY PREMISES

Thomas J. Peters is a business management author, lecturer and expert on personal and business empowerment and problem-solving methodologies. In

1982, he co-authored with Robert H. Waterman, Jr the seminal management text *In Search of Excellence: Lessons from America's Best-Run Companies*. This best-seller, which remains one of the world's most widely read business books, presents the results of the authors' studies of 43 of the *Fortune* 500's top-performing companies and lists the eight common attributes that the authors argue were responsible for those companies' success:

1. Active decision making.

2. Closeness to customers and a desire to learn from them.

3. Autonomy and entrepreneurship – the nurturing of innovation and fostering of 'champions.'

4. Productivity through people – treating all employees as sources of quality.

5. A hands-on, value-driven management approach – management showing its commitment.

6. A focus on what the company does best.

7. A simple form and lean staff – the authors found that some of the best companies had minimal headquarters staff.

8. Balance between a centralized and a decentralized organization, involving autonomy in shop-floor activities combined with centralized values.

Following the publication of *In Search of Excellence*, Peters went on to author or co-author more than a dozen books on business management. He continues to lecture and publish articles on business and personal empowerment and problem solving.

HOW KEY PREMISES CHANGED BUSINESSES AND INCREASED PROJECTS

Tom Peters's theories did not in themselves create many large new projects. However, smaller projects and studies were begun in the eight attributes of success areas.

MENTION OF PROJECT MANAGEMENT AND ITS LINK WITH STRATEGY EXECUTION

Peters did not discuss project management or its link with strategy execution. Although some of the characteristics on his list of eight common attributes of success, such as active decision making, could be related to project management, none of the key findings of his study of top-performing companies mentioned project management or strategy execution.

Michael Eugene Porter (23 May 1947–)

SUMMARY OF KEY PREMISES

Michael Porter has been identified by many surveys as the world's most influential thinker on management and competitiveness. He is the founder of the modern strategy field, and his work has redefined theories about competitiveness, economic development, economically distressed urban communities, environmental policy and the role of corporations in society.

One of Porter's most important contributions was to propose a strategic system through which a firm, or a region, could develop a competitive advantage. This system consists primarily of:

- The five forces analysis, which studies those forces close to a company that affect its ability to serve its customers and make a profit.

- Strategic groups, which are companies within an industry that have similar business models or strategies.

- The value chain, which categorizes an organization's value-added activities. Value-chain analysis examines every step a business goes through – from receiving raw materials, to adding value to these raw materials through various processes and then to selling the finished product to customers.

- The generic strategies of cost leadership, differentiation and focus.

- The market-positioning strategies of value-based, needs-based and access-based marketing.

- Clusters of competence for regional economic development. These clusters comprise such diverse members of the public and private sector as firms, government agencies and academic institutions that join together to work on development projects designed to improve the regional economy.

HOW KEY PREMISES CHANGED BUSINESSES AND INCREASED PROJECTS

Porter changed the way companies look at their businesses and analyse their strategies. However, his theories did not significantly increase the number of projects. Through his value-chain concept he enforced the functional structure of companies, which has become a key challenge for organizations that want to be able to execute their strategic projects.

MENTION OF PROJECT MANAGEMENT AND ITS LINK WITH STRATEGY EXECUTION

Porter does not mention either the importance of project management or the link with strategy execution. Despite the fact that he revolutionized the way companies look at strategy, he surprisingly fails to cover how strategy is executed.

Michael Martin Hammer (13 April 1948–3 September 2008)

SUMMARY OF KEY PREMISES

Michael Hammer is best known for his 1993 book *Reengineering the Corporation*, which he co-authored with James Champy. The book's main argument is that companies should break down their activities into small, logical pieces and then reassemble those pieces in a way that maximizes customer value while minimizing the consumption of resources. This argument builds on Hammer's claim, in a 1990 *Harvard Business Review* article, that most of the work being done in corporations does not add value for the customers and should be eliminated rather than accelerated through automation.[3]

A large number of firms quickly began to review their business processes. They were striving to regain the competitiveness they had lost due to the

---

3   M. Hammer, Reengineering work: Don't automate, obliterate, *Harvard Business Review* (1990).

market entrance of foreign competitors, their inability to satisfy customer needs and their insufficient cost structures. Even well-regarded management gurus such as Peter Drucker and Tom Peters advocated business process engineering (BPR) as a new tool for achieving or regaining success in a changing world. In addition, numerous publications were devoted to discussions of BPR, and many consulting firms developed BPR methods.

Nevertheless, critics claimed that BPR was a way to dehumanize the workplace, increase management control and justify downsizing. Despite these criticisms, however, by 1993 as many as 65 per cent of the *Fortune* 500 companies claimed that they had either initiated reengineering or had plans to do so.

Ultimately, reengineering has earned a poor reputation because such projects have often resulted in massive layoffs. This reputation is not altogether unwarranted, since companies have often downsized under the banner of reengineering.

HOW KEY PREMISES CHANGED BUSINESSES AND INCREASED PROJECTS

Hammer's business process reengineering revolutionized the way modern companies looked at how they were carrying out their work and how they were organized. In most of the world's largest companies, BPR led to an explosion of long and cumbersome projects that required changes in the way employees worked. As a result, a number of people were laid off.

Consulting firms benefited greatly from BPR, introducing the concept to probably all the largest corporations. IT systems were also the focus of BPR, and those projects – some of the largest carried out by corporations in the 1990s – became known as enterprise resource planning (ERP) implementations. Most of the ERP implementation projects were significantly late and greatly over budget, yet probably all the top 500 companies in the world have gone through at least one such implementation.

MENTION OF PROJECT MANAGEMENT AND ITS LINK WITH STRATEGY EXECUTION

Michael Hammer does not specifically refer to project management and its importance to strategy execution. However, his theories significantly increased the number of projects in the business world.

Table 2.1   Management gurus

Business Theories		
Author	Refer to Project Management	Link Strategy and Execution
1 Henry Ford	No	No
2 Frederick Winslow Taylor	No	No
3 Peter Drucker	No	No
4 Michael Eugene Porter	No	No
5 Deming	No	No
6 Mintzberg	No	No
7 Prahalad and Hamel	No	No
8 Hammer and Champy	No	No
9 Kotter and Schlesigner	*Yes*	No
10 Kaplan and Norton	No	No
11 Kruger	No	No

Conclusions

None of the most influential business management gurus referred to project management as an important business methodology or as a critical component of strategy execution. In fact, as shown in Table 2.1, only two of the authors of the top 11 business books listed mention project management at all. This oversight is one of the main reasons why most of today's business leaders continue to ignore the value of project management.

Ignored by Most Top MBA Programmes

After determining that most business management gurus disregard project management and its link with strategy execution, I wanted to find out whether the same was true of the top business schools. Specifically, I wanted know whether the Master of Business Administration (MBA) programmes at such world-renowned institutions as Harvard and INSEAD – which teach the world's future CEOs and senior executives – actually include project management as part of their core business curriculum.

Using the *Financial Times* 2010 ranking of the world's top business schools, in summer/autumn of that year I researched whether any of them taught project management as either a core course or an elective course. As shown

Table 2.2   The top 25 MBAs in the world

SL. No	School Name	Country	Core Project or Programme Management	Electives Project or Programme
1	London Business School	UK	No	Yes
2	University of Pennsylvania: Wharton	USA	No	No
3	Harvard Business School	USA	No	No
4	Stanford University GSB	USA	No	No
5	INSEAD	France/Singapore	No	No
6	Columbia Business School	USA	No	No
7	IE Business School	Spain	No	No
8	MIT Sloan School of Management	USA	No	No
9	University of Chicago: Booth	USA	No	No
10	Hong Kong UST Business School	China	No	No
11	Iese Business School	Spain	No	No
12	Indian School of Business	India	No	No
13	New York University: Stern	USA	No	No
14	Dartmouth College: Tuck	USA	No	No
15	IMD	Switzerland	No	No
16	Yale School of Management	USA	No	No
17	University of Oxford: Said	UK	No	No
18	HEC Paris	France	No	No
19	Esade Business School	Spain	No	No
20	Duke University: Fuqua	USA	No	No
21	University of Cambridge: Judge	UK	No	No
22	Ceibs	China	No	Yes
23	Northwestern University: Kellogg	USA	No	No
24	Lancaster University Management School	UK	No	No
25	Rotterdam School of Management, Erasmus University	Netherlands	No	No

in Table 2.2, the results were astonishing. At the time only two of the top 100 MBA programmes in the world taught project management as a core course: the UK's Cranfield School of Management,[4] which was ranked 26th in the world; and the University of Iowa's Tippie College of Business,[5] ranked 64th in the world. However, if we look at the business schools that offer project management as an elective course the number increases significantly – to 28 out of the top 100 schools.[6]

Not Yet Considered a Top Discipline by the Preeminent Strategy Consulting Firms

After reviewing the theories of the major business management gurus and the curricula at the top business schools, I turned my attention to the world's three biggest, most prestigious and most admired strategy consulting firms. All three firms – McKinsey & Company, Bain & Company and The Boston Consulting Group (BCG) – provide advice to most of the CEOs and senior executives of the *Fortune* 1,000 multinationals in the western world. I was interested in finding out whether they provide specific project management and/or strategy execution advisory services.

MCKINSEY & COMPANY

McKinsey & Company is the most influential strategy consulting firm in the world, advising more than 70 per cent of *Fortune* magazine's list of most-admired companies. I examined the firm's website,[7] assuming that project management-related services would be offered; but that was not the case. Although McKinsey makes its living through projects – each of its assignments is essentially a project – the company does not offer its clients any advice on project management, prioritization or execution.

BAIN & COMPANY

Bain & Company claims that through using its advice clients have historically outperformed the stock market by 4:1. Bain was founded in 1973 on the

---

4   Details available at http://www.som.cranfield.ac.uk/som/p786/Programmes-and-Executive-Development/MBA/your-mba-programme/The-Cranfield-MBA-Programme-structure.
5   See http://tippie.uiowa.edu/fulltimemba/academics/corecourses.cfm.
6   The two business schools that teach project management as core courses also offer these courses as electives.
7   See http://www.mckinsey.com/clientservice/functional.asp#midpage.

principle that consultants should deliver results – not just reports – to their clients. Nevertheless, the company's website[8] did not include a section on project management when consulted.

THE BOSTON CONSULTING GROUP

The Boston Consulting Group helps clients deliver customized solutions that resolve their most significant issues and create lasting competitive advantage. Yet, again, this leading strategy consulting firm's website failed to list project management as a major capability.[9] However, unlike McKinsey and Bain, BCG does offer project management advisory services. Under the caption 'Operations' I found a section entitled 'program management.' Because, as discussed in Chapter 1, operations are the opposite of project management, this is not the best way to categorize this service; but at least it is offered.

Overall, consulting firms are not big champions of project management with CEOs; but this is perfectly understandable based on previous findings.

Discounted as a Key Topic by the Finest Business Publications

Despite all of my findings indicating that project management has been ignored, I decided to complete one last piece of research before drawing conclusions. This involved reviewing *McKinsey Quarterly* and the *Harvard Business Review* to see how these top business publications cover the topic of project management and its link with strategy execution.

McKinsey Quarterly was founded in 1964 by McKinsey & Company and is targeted at chief executives, top managers and selected academics. Its articles are written by McKinsey consultants to offer practical suggestions culled from their experience with the world's largest companies. Initially the *Quarterly* was distributed by the McKinsey partners but it is now distributed electronically. My review of the list of functions on the online version of *McKinsey Quarterly*[10] revealed many familiar ones, but none related to project management or strategy execution. Does this mean that these two topics are not sufficiently relevant?

---

8   See http://www.bain.com/bainweb/Consulting_Expertise/capabilities_overview.asp.
9   See http://www.bcg.com/expertise_impact/capabilities/default.aspx.
10 See http://www.mckinseyquarterly.com/home.aspx.

Table 2.3   Number of references/articles per topic *Harvard Business Review* (7 March 2011)

	Topic	References
1	Strategy	6,515
2	Marketing	5,954
3	Finance	5,528
4	Organizational behaviour	5,427
5	Human resource management	5,374
6	Leadership	4,674
7	Operations management	3,492
8	Information technology	3,428
9	Global business	2,973
10	Business and government relations	2,777
11	Innovation	2,606
12	Accounting	2,516
13	Organizational change	2,355
14	Business ethics	2,248
15	Entrepreneurship	2,088
16	Competition	1,909
17	Change management	1,774
18	Decision making	1,431
19	Mergers and acquisitions	1,369
20	Negotiation	1,289
21	Sales	1,225
22	Implementing strategy	1,203
23	Career planning	947
24	Economics	917
25	Corporate governance	761
26	Psychology	591
27	Employee retention	558
28	Project management	432
29	Financial markets	375
30	New economy	337

The *Harvard Business Review* is considered the bible in terms of business management thinking and new trends. First published in 1922 by Harvard University, its mission is to improve the practice of project management and its impact on changing the world. In 2010, the *Review* had a circulation of

236,000. The results of my review of the publication's website[11] to determine the topics mentioned and the number of references to each topic are shown in Table 2.3.

Clearly, this shows that the key topics written about in the *Harvard Business Review* are those most addressed by business gurus – which in turn are the subjects taught most frequently at the top business schools and discussed most often by leading consultants. Only 432 of its articles have been written about project management, which represent less than 0.5 per cent of the total number of articles published. Strategy execution – or 'implementation,' as the publication calls it – is the subject of a somewhat greater number of articles (1,203); but both topics are far from the top of the list.

Finally, every year McKinsey gives an award to the two best articles published in the *Harvard Business Review*. This award, judged by an independent panel of leaders in the business community, recognizes outstanding works that are likely to have a major influence on the actions of business managers worldwide. A review of all of the winners of the McKinsey award since 1959 provides a history lesson on the development of management thinking. None of the 51 winning articles has related to project management or strategy execution.

Conclusions

My research shows very clearly why project management has not been relevant and the consequent disregard of this discipline by senior leaders. For most of the project management community, this is a very painful discovery; but it helps to understand the reasons for this indifference. For many strategists, this lack of awareness of the importance of project management explains the problems with strategy execution. Only when project management is recognized as being vital to strategy execution will companies begin to more effectively achieve their goals.

---

11 See http://www.hbr.com.

3

Why So Many Strategic Initiatives Have Failed

During the past century, companies' efforts to achieve their strategic initiatives have led to the relentless improvement, and thus constant reduction, of operational work (run-the-business activities) and to an unstoppable increase in projects (change-the-business activities). This slow but inevitable trend has had a significant impact on strategy execution. Unfortunately many companies remain ill-equipped to manage this shift. Therefore, as the number of projects multiplied, the rate of strategic failures increased. My research shows that the traditional functional company's poor project management skills – and the resulting difficulties in executing its strategy – can be linked to seven main obstacles:

1. Omission of uniform methods and standard processes.

2. Misalignment of organizational structure with the company's changing reality.

3. Absence of appropriate governing structure to support strategy execution.

4. Lack of project execution culture, skills and leadership attention.

5. Complexity of tracking and forecasting project costs, financials and benefits.

6. Inadequacy of systems and tools for monitoring strategy execution.

7. Lack of focus.

Omission of Uniform Methods and Standard Processes

PROJECT MANAGEMENT

Project management can be viewed as an organized set of processes that bring order and efficiency to the work and team management of any size project that has a definable end. Therefore, the existence of well-defined project management methods and processes – referred to as the project management methodology – identifies those companies that have the best chance to consistently deliver project results. Project management is similar to such business processes as supply chain, logistics, finance and strategic planning.

For many decades, as seen in the Spare Parts Benny, Inc. case study, companies lacked a common and standard approach for managing projects. First, the recognition and establishment of the role of project manager took many years; then each project manager had their own way of documenting a project's key elements. Some managers used, for example, a Microsoft® (MS) Word document; others used PowerPoint; and still others used Excel, making project comparison and follow-up impossible tasks. Research I carried out in 2005 showed that over 80 per cent of the 200 companies I reviewed were using MS Office applications (including MS Project) to manage their projects.

Further, projects were often initiated without a detailed business case – sometimes even with just an email. Many companies were using shareholders' money to invest in expensive projects that had not been analysed thoroughly. Project costs were not only poorly defined before they started but also were not properly tracked once the project began. To make matters worse, often a department would launch a new project only to find out later that another department within the same company had launched a similar project. With no uniform methodology or processes, companies were unable to effectively execute and document key aspects of a project.

PROJECT PORTFOLIO MANAGEMENT

In addition to missing a uniform project management methodology, companies had no standard way of selecting and prioritizing project ideas – which in project management terms is called project portfolio management (PPM) and is the engine for the change-the-business activities.

One of top management's critical tasks is to select projects in which to invest, ensuring that they are aligned to the strategy; they bring enough value to achieve the company's objectives; and that they are systematically executed until their completion and their benefits are achieved. Even more important for top management is to decide on which initiatives they will not fund or those they will stop. As will be discussed later, saying 'no' is a key characteristic of becoming a focused organization.

Next, management must prioritize the selected projects, always being aware of the top three to five projects that will bring the company closer to its strategic goals. Being unaware of which projects are most important for the company is one of the key reasons for employees' lack of focus and therefore strategic failure.

A number of years ago, companies began setting up efficient project management methodologies and implementing beneficial changes in organizational governance. Project portfolio management is a more cumbersome change, which only a few companies have managed to master. The second part of this book will cover the best ways to develop and implement project management and portfolio management methodology.

Misalignment of Organizational Structure with the Company's Changing Reality

In his book *Strategy and Structure*, published in 1962, Alfred Chandler claims that an organization's structure should be driven by its chosen strategy; otherwise, the result is inefficiency. Taking this one step further, the alignment and balance of the organizational structure with the degree to which change-the-business activities are important determines overall project performance and strategy execution success. More often than not, management underestimates or completely ignores this fact, organizations fail to evolve (or adapt) as quickly as the business drivers and consequently a large proportion of projects fail.

Chapter 1 discussed the fact that most companies have been structured functionally – ideal for run-the-business activities, with departments divided along a value chain influenced by Michael Porter's model. Traditional companies are generally run by a chief executive officer (CEO), a chief finance officer (CFO) and often a chief operations officer (COO) and a chief information officer (CIO) – the 'C-suite' – followed by the heads of each functional department; and each department has had its own budget and resources.

Until recently, departmental success was measured using key performance indicators tailored to each function. For example, the finance department's success was measured by whether it was closing the books and producing financial statements on time, and the human resources (HR) department by whether it had managed to keep good personnel on board (low turnover) or had finished all employee appraisals by the deadline.

This approach created lots of internal competition and a 'silo mentality.' Some heads of departments built their own little empires and cooperation with other parts of the business became very difficult. In many cases, the key performance indicators of one department could be at odds with those of another.

At the same time, the largest and most critical projects – the strategic ones – are almost always cross-departmental. This means that a strategic project such as expanding the business into another country requires resources and input from a number of different departments:

- Facility experts find the location.

- Lawyers handle the legal documents.

- HR experts recruit the staff.

- Salespeople develop a commercial plan and so forth.

Without the contribution of all these departments the project would not succeed. Cross-departmental – or companywide – projects in a traditional, functional organization always faced the same difficulties, some of which are outlined below.

WHICH DEPARTMENT WILL LEAD THE PROJECT?

With a major strategic project, generally two or three department heads would volunteer to take the lead since they would gain a substantial career boost if the project were successful. The contrary was also true – as, for example, with the never-ending enterprise resource planning (ERP) implementations in the late 1990s. The most common conflicts are between the business and the information technology (IT) departments.

WHO WILL BE THE PROJECT MANAGER?

The project manager plays a critical role in the project's success. Despite any organizational difficulties, this person can really make a difference. A good project manager can:

- Navigate the organization.

- Motivate the team.

- Sell the project benefits throughout the company.

- Deliver on scope, on time and within budget.

Unfortunately, good project managers are scarce and because companies have many strategic projects, such projects are often led by managers who lack all the necessary qualifications.

In a traditional, functional, run-the-business organization a department with a good project manager will never be easily convinced to lend him or her to manage another department's project, for three main reasons:

1.   If the project is successful, the credit will go to the head of the other department.

2.   If a new strategic project begins in the project manager's original department, the best project manager will no longer be available.

3.   Even if the 'loaned' project manager is able to arrange for resources to be allocated to the project, they still report to their functional boss. This may lead to time-consuming negotiations between the project manager and department heads to keep people on the project team, which wastes energy and slows down the project – sometimes even causing it to fail.

WHO WILL SPONSOR THE PROJECT?

Deciding who will sponsor the project has always been difficult, particularly for those projects which, if successful, provide the sponsor with a career jump. For example, with the start of e-commerce in the late 1990s many department heads wanted to take the lead, which often caused disagreement between the CIO and the marketing manager.

HOW IS A MULTIDISCIPLINARY TEAM SELECTED AND HOW IS THEIR DEDICATION TO THE PROJECT OBTAINED?

Selecting the members of a companywide, multidisciplinary team, similar to choosing the project manager, is always a difficult task – and for two main reasons:

1.   The best people, the experts, are usually overbooked.

2.   Most of the project members have their own day-to-day operational responsibilities, so the time they can give to a project is often limited.

The consequence here, as previously discussed, is that some strategic projects end up being run by less experienced and lower quality staff. The second part of this book will discuss why successful strategy execution depends on having the best people run the most strategic projects.

WHO 'OWNS' THE RESOURCES ASSIGNED TO THE PROJECT?

Most of the resources (personnel) who work on projects report to a line/functional manager and thus are part of the run-the-business dimension. The line/functional manager needs to ensure that his/her staff are occupied full time. Project managers do not 'own' resources; they need to ask the line/functional managers to 'lend' some of their experts to contribute to the project. Often resources are assigned on a part-time basis, but two part-time resources will never perform as one fully dedicated person. In addition, the priorities of the line/functional manager can change midway through a project and it is possible that they will need the resource(s) back. The fact that resources are owned mainly by the run-the-business side can create a lot of conflict in projects.

WHO PAYS FOR THE PROJECT?

Determining who will pay for the project has been a major problem since the beginning of modern project management in the 1970s. As will be explained later in this chapter, management of a company's finances and budgets is strongly linked to its organizational structure. Consequently, allocating budgets and tracking costs by projects rather than by functions is a highly cumbersome exercise. Adding to this complexity is the 'silo mentality,' with managers often wondering why they should commit resources and a budget to a project that, although important, would give them no credit if successful. Rather, a management colleague – often a direct competitor – would benefit.

As will be explained later, a silo mentality can be overcome by giving more weight and power to companywide project management.

Cross-functional (strategic) projects always require a negotiation phase before they begin. Companies with a clear project execution process are able to quickly get through this phase and execute their projects because they have dedicated, and preferably the best, resources available, quick decision-making capability and total commitment from management.

Within the traditional functional organizational structure, however, quick project execution is not possible. Managing just one project in such a company is already complex, so imagine the difficulty of selecting and executing hundreds of different sized projects.

To summarize, almost all the power in a traditional functional organization – namely resources, budgets and decision making – still resides with the functional/department heads. However, the most important and strategic projects have become cross-departmental, requiring the sharing of that power among other members of the organization in the pursuit of what is best for the business.

Absence of Appropriate Governing Structure to Support Strategy Execution

Another important reason why traditional functional organizations have difficulty supporting and following up on strategy execution is the absence of the right governing structure.

Once the strategic planning department has consolidated the strategic plans for the next three to five years, it hands over the execution to the different departments. As previously noted, departments within functional organizations concentrate only on the portion of the strategy for which they are responsible. For example, marketing will focus almost exclusively on its marketing plan, which in turn will be broken down into different initiatives, programmes and projects. But today's governing structure requires finding someone (a role or a department) to take responsibility for:

- Cross-departmental projects – which are often the most strategic.

- A consolidated overview of the progress of strategy execution. This function will follow up on cases and raise a red flag where strategy is not being executed correctly.

Although the CEO, together with the executive board, is ultimately responsible for all company initiatives, today most companies lack clearly assigned responsibilities for effective companywide strategy execution, and thus such initiatives often fail. My recent research showed that only 52 per cent of the companies observed had an established project management department; and only 23 per cent had a project portfolio management office, which – as explained earlier – is the engine that should coordinate the company's entire change-the-business dimension.

A project management office (PMO), on the other hand, is a small unit whose main mission is to follow up and report on the progress of all projects under its scope. The PMO originated in the 1960s – when it was called a project support office (PSO) – and was set up to help with large, complex aerospace and construction projects. Over the years, PSOs were adopted by telecommunications and similar industries and were also used to support project management automated tools such as the Artemis scheduling system.

The use of PSOs really expanded in the 1990s with the first wave of enterprise resource planning[1] implementations, which were among the most complex companywide projects. To date, almost all ERP projects have run late – not by just a few months but rather by several years. The same is true for

---

1   Enterprise resource planning systems (ERPs) was a term originally used for the inventory management and control applications developed in the 1960s. A decade later, these systems evolved into what was called material requirements planning (MRP) and the distribution resource planning (DRP) systems, which automated all aspects of production scheduling and inventory planning. In the 1980s, predecessors of ERPs evolved into the manufacturing resource planning (MRP II) applications and covered business processes other than production, such as front- and back-office processes – distribution, finance, human resources. The MRP IIs became what is today known as ERPs, which can be considered enterprise-wide information systems. ERPs, which include market leaders SAP and Oracle, are customized module software that can handle most of organizations' information system requirements. They are transaction-oriented rather than project-oriented processing systems.

costs, with initial budget overruns of more than 1,000 per cent. It is widely known that companies such as Boeing, Apple, Dow Chemicals and Exxon have all experienced disastrous ERP projects. Some companies, for example FoxMeyer, have even accused their ERP vendors of causing their bankruptcy.

All of the ERP implementations required external consultants with very different skills, one of which was setting up and running the project support office. The PSO performed administrative and bureaucratic tasks such as collecting consultants' weekly timesheets or storing the project documentation. Because ERP projects took many years, PSOs also took on the coordination of other projects: first, to ensure follow-up and reporting; and, second, to ensure consistency in project management practices.

By the mid-1990s the PSO had evolved into the programme/project management office (PMO). In most cases the PMO was situated in the IT department, mainly because its role had evolved to provide support across a variety of projects that were driven most often by IT.[2] Given its location, the PMO was often run by the IT director or chief information officer.

As the PMO's scope and activities[3] increased, so did the number of people in the office. In addition, transparency improved because once the PMO was well established, it provided a good picture of where all projects stood – not only IT but also business and strategic projects.

Because business departments were not yet implementing PMOs they lacked an overview of the effectiveness of the company's entire portfolio of projects.

---

2 Standish Group estimates that deploying a project management office can reduce project failures by up to 80 per cent. *The Chaos Report* (1995), The Standish Group. See http://www. standishgroup.com.

3 Activities that can be performed within a PMO:

- help management select and prioritize projects that support strategic goals;
- facilitate companywide project coordination and consistency;
- set common standards, methodologies, templates and tools for project and portfolio management;
- allocate resources by identifying who is available to work on upcoming projects;
- by developing KPIs, monitor and report on the progress of the entire project portfolio;
- support the project management community with coaching, training and career development;
- collect and archive the documents from completed projects and analyse them for trends;
- develop a knowledge management tool to gather all project-related information
- perform project management quality audits of the projects.

Soon, however, the entire management team understood the importance of the PMO as a source of valuable information for the organization. Battles began for control of PMOs, and the need for a clear governing structure for the company's strategy execution became even more apparent. Chapter's 5 and 6 in the second part of this book explain how the PMO can become the CEO's driver and eyes with regard to a company's strategy execution.

Lack of Project Execution Culture, Skills and Leadership Attention

Many companies lack a clear execution culture, an omission closely linked to the fact that many senior executives ignore the full potential of project management. Without the proper mindset among leadership teams, strategies are doomed to failure. The lack of execution culture and the minor importance given to project management are reflected in several ways, as outlined below.

PROJECT MANAGEMENT IS NOT CONSIDERED A CORE COMPETENCY

Most companies do not regard project management as a strategic skill that has to be nurtured and developed. Rather, it is considered to be something technical and therefore only needed by the IT or engineering departments – and in fact there are only few signs of change. For example, Philips, the Dutch appliances multinational, requires its employees to spend one year managing a project before they can be considered for vice president level. Procter & Gamble too requires key staff to spend a couple of years managing projects if they want to climb the career ladder.

ABSENCE OF CAREER PATHS FOR PROJECT MANAGERS

The chances of a project manager becoming CEO of the company are close to zero. Instead, this position is more likely to be filled by marketing, sales or finance personnel. Companies lack a clear career path for staff working on projects. My latest survey showed that only one in four companies had a clearly defined career path for their change-the-business staff (which was just implemented). Despite the fact that a project team member might become a project manager, project leader, programme manager and programme director, this progression is not linked to a career path that leads to head of the company. A company's career path is solely oriented toward the run-the-business dimension.

LACK OF TRAINING FOR SENIOR MANAGEMENT

Very few companies provide training for their senior managers on strategy execution and the key principles of project and portfolio management. Most training available in companies are on run-the-business activities. Today, many decision makers are unaware of the key principles of their project management methodologies; they do not know what is expected of them during a project; and they do not understand the concept of portfolio management.

FAILURE TO LINK INCENTIVES TO PROJECT RESULTS

Another indication of the neglect of project management is that companies almost never link incentives to project results. This is true not only for project managers and team members but also for senior managers who make the decisions about which projects to invest in and sponsor. Instead, performance objectives and incentives are most often linked to operational and functional roles (run-the-business activities). Thus, in order to meet their targets and earn their bonuses, employees continue to put most of their efforts into these roles. To make matters worse, project managers are generally paid less than sales, marketing or even finance staff.

CULTURAL DIFFERENCES, SILO MENTALITIES AND INTERNAL COMPETITION

The lack of a single focused and strong execution culture creates an excess of cultures within the same company. One consequence of this can be that in a multinational company different cultural traditions and belief systems can cause behavioural conflicts and misunderstandings. As shown by Geert Hofstede, people behave and make decisions based on the values of their home countries.[4]

Another result of this lack of execution culture is that departments create their own culture 'silo' which does not necessarily consider what is best for the entire company. This creates much conflict and negative internal competition, which is transmitted to the staff.

This abundance of cultures, and the problems that can result, must be addressed if the company wants to perform optimally. These issues will be examined later in the book, when how to develop a winning execution culture is discussed.

---

4   See http://www.geert-hofstede.com.

Complexity of Tracking and Forecasting Project Costs, Financials and Benefits

The complexity of clarifying the related finances and budgets is one reason why project management's value is so often underestimated. Executives like to have reliable information (and not just data) in order to make the best decisions; but, as I will explain next, this is one of the most problematic and least mature aspects of project management. Not only is tracking project costs extremely cumbersome but measuring the benefits of investments is also a tortuous exercise. In the end, project management and change-the-business activities are far from being exact sciences. To make matters even worse, as we will see later, companies' budgeting processes and systems have been developed and are applied to the run-the-business dimension.

IMPOSSIBILITY OF PRECISELY TRACKING EMPLOYEES' PROJECT WORK

Calculating precisely the level of staff and financial resources that companies dedicate to and invest in change-the-business activities (projects) is a huge challenge. The most important component of such a calculation is the time that employees dedicate to working on their assigned portion of the overall project. However, in most businesses employees spend only part of their time working on projects, with the remainder spent continuing their operational work (e.g., a marketing expert may be part of a project team for a few days a week but will continue their marketing activities the rest of the time).[5] The fact that employees often work on several projects simultaneously adds further complexity to the accurate tracking of project costs.

So how can companies know precisely how much time each employee has spent on an assigned activity? Even if an employee is scheduled to work two days a week on a project, the calculation is often imprecise. The answer proposed by today's most advanced project management systems is to use a timesheet. In principle this is not a bad solution but in reality:

- Very few employees actually like to fill out timesheets.

- Senior management, who are the project sponsors and members of the steering committees, almost never fill out timesheets.

---

5   The exceptions here are organizations such as consulting firms, which make a living completing projects, or companies that dedicate resources full time to one specific project.

- IT and engineering personnel may be highly disciplined but, overall, timesheet accuracy is never 100 per cent.

Thus, if most timesheets are not filled out – and if the ones that *are* completed are inaccurate – there is still no way of knowing the exact cost of one project, let alone the hundreds of projects that a company typically completes. Some recent articles have stated that in the future timesheets will be replaced by biometric applications,[6] which may be a move in the right direction but will take years to implement.

Another problem with trying to accurately track employees' project work is that most companies outsource a portion of the project to consulting companies for a fixed price. The method of recording these costs is different from that used with timesheets. In addition, projects involve unique expenses such as hardware and software licenses, which sometimes must be amortized. In the end, all of these variables make the cost calculation very complex. Sometimes project managers spend more time trying to incorporate all these calculations into their business case planning and follow-up than actually managing the project.

FAILURE TO IDENTIFY AND MEASURE PROJECT BENEFITS

Probably one of the biggest pitfalls in project management is its inability to clearly track the benefits delivered by the projects. In principle, a solid project management culture should help a company achieve its strategic objectives. Yet, in reality, most of the project benefits as described in the initial business case are hardly ever tracked. The main reasons why tracking benefits is so difficult are:

- Project benefits are often reaped months or years after the project has been finished (e.g., the synergies in a merger are often spread over three to five years).

- Companies have neither a department nor function that is responsible for tracking the benefits. During the execution, the sponsor is accountable for the project. After the project's completion, that accountability ends.

- When projects are completed, their deliverable is transferred to the run-the-business activities, where accountability for the project disappears.

---

6   Examples of biometric applications can be found at http://www.bio-metrica.com.

- No systems or tools currently exist that specialize in tracking project benefits; thus, there is no formal way to follow up on strategy execution.

- Much has been written about benefits management, which is a project management term introduced less than a decade ago. It created a lot of hype for a while but today very few companies have implemented the process, and probably none have mastered it.

FAILURE OF THE BUDGETING CYCLE TO ADDRESS PROJECT EXECUTION

The budgeting cycle involves forecasting a business's revenues and expenses, generally for the coming year. Forecasting is used to control spending, ensure that funds are available and used according to plan and keep spending within preset limits.

Every year, each department's head estimates costs and revenues for the coming year. Top management usually provides guidance to the different entities in the form of target expectations. For example, one instruction could be that all fixed costs for the next year need to be reduced by 2.3 per cent. After several iterations, the budget is approved by the executive team. Once the forecast is in place, quarterly meetings are held to review actual spending and reconfirm the forecast for the rest of the year. The budgeting cycle, which is mandatory in every company and has been in place for decades, is led by the finance department.

Unfortunately, the traditional budgeting cycle is not aware of, and thus does not take into account, the distinction between run-the-business activities and change-the-business activities. Thus, the link between budgeting cycles and project activities is fraught with obstacles. First, there is a discrepancy in timing. The traditional budgeting cycle estimates costs for the year to come (i.e., a business will budget for 2012 in 2011), whereas projects are multiyear, often lasting for a number of years. Because businesses must follow the traditional budget, project budgets are never fully captured and are often completely ignored.

Second, project costs are not one of the elements of a traditional budget and forecast. Rather, the traditional categories are:

- Profit and loss.

- Balance sheet.

- Capital expenditures (CAPEX) – can be direct and indirect.

- Operational expenditures (OPEX).

- Staff expenses.

- Management costs.

- FTE evolution.

Almost of all of these elements are associated with run-the-business activities. The closest a traditional budget gets to accounting for change-the-business costs is within the CAPEX category, but these expenditures are limited to investments in fixed assets (e.g., buildings, IT equipment, software). Not all of the investments in projects can be capitalized. The rules for project cost depreciation are often confused. Therefore, creating a project budget involves collecting information from different sources; and often this information is neither straightforward nor 100 per cent reliable.

In addition, very few companies create a budget for companywide change-the-business activities. Some companies forecast project costs by department, but rarely do they develop a budget for projects that are in the best interests of the entire company.

The prioritization of new projects, which should be completed annually as part of the budgeting cycle, is an arduous exercise with many assumptions. This is yet another clear example that the business world is structured to deal with run-the-business activities and has not yet adapted to the silent trend described in Chapter 1.

LACK OF ATTENTION TO PROJECT INVESTMENTS BY COMPANY, SHAREHOLDERS, BOARDS AND FINANCIAL ANALYSTS

It is surprising that company shareholders, boards and even financial analysts do not demand much information about the key strategic projects and change-the-business activities their company has invested in and their subsequent execution status. Any attention paid to projects seems to happen only when a business is about to engage in a large acquisition. In this case, management speaks to company shareholders either to ask their approval and/or to raise capital to complete the acquisition.[7] The company makes a business case for the anticipated costs and synergies, which then are made public. After the acquisition has taken place, financial analysts and shareholders follow up regularly.

Other than in cases of large acquisitions, CEOs and senior executives do not give projects much attention. If investments in, and the execution of, projects are not scrutinized, then they are clearly not a priority. There are a very few exceptions – such as in the pharmaceutical or oil and gas industries – where analysts and shareholders do try to find out about such companies' new strategic projects such as new blockbuster drugs or new petroleum drillings.

NEGLECT OF PROJECT REPORTING BY ACCOUNTING STANDARDS AND AUDIT FIRMS

Another interesting finding is that neither of the two most important sets of accounting standards specifies clearly how companies should report on their projects and their change-the-business activities. Both the United States Generally Accepted Accounting Principles (US GAAP) and the International Accounting Standards (IAS) fail to include a codification topic covering how to account for project costs and how to report project benefits. The closest they get to mentioning project reporting is a discussion of development costs that should be amortized (US GAAP 350-50/IAS 38).

The lack of clear project standards is also reflected in the work of the big audit firms such as PricewaterhouseCoopers or KPMG. In fact, projects are not addressed during the companies' required annual audits. How is it possible that auditors do not audit the hundreds of projects that a company might be running, perhaps involving 35 per cent of the staff, and use the results as input in issuing their opinion?

All of these oversights are ultimately reflected in the company's annual reports, in which hardly any reference is made to the projects that the company has invested in and how they link to strategic objectives. This omission is difficult to understand because the value and future growth of a company will

---

7   In a recent case, the former Belgian bank Fortis asked approval of its shareholders to acquire the Dutch bank ABN AMRO in a consortium with two other banks (see Chapter 1).

be determined primarily by its investment decisions and its ability to execute those decisions. Again, projects are not given high priority.

All the points mentioned above with respect to the budgeting and forecasting cycle are clear evidence that companies and their key elements are structured in a functional way to deal with the run-the-business activities. In the second part of this book I will explain how to address the resulting gaps.

Inadequacy of Systems and Tools for Monitoring Strategy Execution

In the 1990s, companies' major IT investment was in ERP systems, with the focus mainly on improving and automating the run-the-business activities (both core operations and supporting activities). At the beginning of the twenty-first century this focus shifted to the Internet and e-commerce. Lately, however, organizations have shown increased interest in specialized project and portfolio management software, confirming a slow movement toward project management as a tool to run their businesses and to execute their strategy. Soon there will likely be a new wave of companywide software implementations to improve and automate organizations' change-the-business activities (project management and portfolio management activities).

The full benefits of this move will likely require five to ten years to be realized. Until recently most companies lacked integrated software to manage their hundreds of projects. The most advanced companies were using Microsoft Project, but often just to describe the project plan and its main milestones. Individual projects were not connected; a consolidated view of the portfolio of projects required information from multiple systems; and up-to-date project information was impossible to obtain.

Consider this real situation: A bank with 540 current projects costing approximately €256 million and involving 4,780 out of 20,000 employees has no tool with which to monitor the projects' status, costs or contributions to strategy execution. Given that the bank has no way of knowing how its portfolio of projects is doing, how can it make good project-related or investment decisions?

As recent as around 2008, project and portfolio management was on the back burner for most companies. Even worse, most companies were unable to monitor their strategy execution because they lacked the tools to follow up on their projects and their change-the-business activities. Only with the rise of programme management offices did some transparency enter this process, soon to be followed by a new wave of project portfolio management software. This software will be discussed in the second part of the book.

Lack of Focus

All the issues discussed in this chapter lead to extremely unfocused companies. Lack of focus has been one of companies' main hindrances in achieving their strategies. Research suggests three main reasons why a company becomes unfocused:

1. Top executives do not know their own company's key strategic initiatives.

2. Being focused is difficult and requires lots of discipline.

3. Finishing projects is very difficult and consequently the number of projects continues to increase.

TOP EXECUTIVES DO NOT KNOW THEIR OWN COMPANY'S KEY STRATEGIC INITIATIVES

I have facilitated more than 30 workshops with senior management teams, during which I ask them to write down their company's top three initiatives and then list their replies on a flipchart. Every time, the responses include more than three initiatives – often far more, and sometimes only the managers' own initiatives. When I reveal the lists there is a moment of silence and a certain level of embarrassment.[8] The point of the exercise, I explain, is to show that if the executives of the firm do not know the company's priorities and are unable to focus on what is key, then they cannot expect this focus from their employees.

This lack of focus can also be explained by the pressure on many CEOs to show results quickly. Consequently, they often invest in many initiatives, thinking they will increase their chances of success. I will show in the second part of this book why this thinking is totally wrong.

---

8   I suggest that you complete this exercise in your own company, you will be astonished with the results.

BEING FOCUSED IS DIFFICULT AND REQUIRES LOTS OF DISCIPLINE

Very closely related to the previous point are the results of a recent Harvard University study which shows that human beings are by nature unfocused.[9] At any given point, on average 50 per cent of the population are not focused on what they are doing. In addition, 30–40 per cent of employees' time in the workplace is spent on unplanned interruptions and then on restoring the mental focus disturbed by these interruptions. This was not the case 20 years ago, simply because the tools of interruption were less plentiful.

Lack of focus leads not only to unhappiness but also to:

- Errors.

- Wasted time.

- Miscommunication and misunderstanding.

- Reduced productivity.

- Loss of revenues.

Focus imposes order. It requires energy, work and some pain, which people often try to avoid. If a company's top management is not focused, this significantly increases the possibility that the rest of the organization is unfocused. On the other hand, and as we will see later, when top management is extremely focused this is transmitted to the staff and the improvement in performance is huge.

STOPPING PROJECTS IS VERY DIFFICULT AND CONSEQUENTLY THE NUMBER OF PROJECTS CONTINUES TO INCREASE

Most companies have trouble cancelling projects that are not doing well. In my entire career I have only seen a few projects terminated – and then only because the company went bankrupt.

One reason why companies find it difficult to end projects is because they do not want to admit they have failed. Most projects have a senior executive

---

9   Study by Daniel Gilbert and Matthew Killingsworth of 250,000 respondents, cited in *New York Times*, 15 November 2010.

as a sponsor, so stopping a project will be seen as their personal failure. This sense of personal failure contributes to the increase in projects and the gradual decrease in focus within the entire organization.

But, as we will see later in the book, all these issues can be overcome. For example, one of the first things that Steve Jobs did when he returned to Apple in 1997 was to cancel, almost immediately, 300 projects. He was convinced that Apple was unfocused and in order to survive, the company had to become *highly* focused. As I will show, the benefits of becoming a focused organization are massive.

PART II

The Benefits and Methods of Becoming Focused

4

How Companies Can FOCUS

Part II of this book explains in practical details the benefits and methods of becoming a focused organization and how this process can help companies successfully execute their strategies.

Elements of Successful Strategy Execution

In today's world, *most companies have very similar strategic objectives*: to find ways to achieve sustainable growth that creates value for their shareholders while keeping costs down. The detailed objectives and the way they are achieved might be slightly different for each company, depending on the chief executive officer' s (CEO's) level of ambition; but in the end, there are not many different options. In addition, most large companies are advised by the same strategic consulting firms – mainly McKinsey & Company, the Boston Consulting Group (BCG) and Bain. These firms use similar methods and industry knowledge that they have acquired over the years, which reinforces the evidence that companies define their strategies in similar ways. Looking at this very simplistically, the fundamental difference between success and failure depends on which projects top management decides to invest in and how those projects are executed.

In other words, finding ways to achieve the strategic goals is what today is known as 'strategic planning,' while 'strategy execution' is the method used to achieve those goals. The three most important elements of successful strategy execution are:

- Identifying the company's core competencies that will differentiate it from the competition.

- Selecting and prioritizing the initiatives that will exploit those core competencies and create sustainable growth via the company's strategic plan.

- Organizing company resources so as to optimally execute the chosen strategy.

SELECTING AND PRIORITIZING INITIATIVES THAT WILL ACHIEVE THE STRATEGY

Most strategic initiatives concentrate on either growth (and are externally focused) or productivity (and are internally focused). The most important components of strategic initiatives are:

- Product, service, and technological innovation.

- Continued growth, for example, through acquisition and international expansion.

- Customer retention and loyalty via repeat purchases.

- Performance improvement.

- Cost control.

Selecting the appropriate initiatives improves all these elements and brings a company closer to successful strategy execution. Part of this process involves management decisions on where to invest company resources based on solid understanding and best use of core competencies. They cannot invest in everything, and choosing which projects to fund can sometimes be a gamble. Top management must also prioritize the projects since not everything can be high priority, and this can involve challenging decision making. Focused companies choose the right projects in which to invest and carry them out in order of importance.

ORGANIZING COMPANY RESOURCES TO SUPPORT EXECUTION

Once the initiatives have been selected and prioritized, the next step is to organize company resources to support the strategy execution. Management should determine early on the right balance between change-the-business and run-the-business activities and whether the company has enough resources and the right capabilities to carry out the selected strategy.

This stage is very similar to what football coaches have to do at the beginning of each season. The team chairmen and the fans set the objectives for the year, but the coaches need to establish whether or not they have the right players to achieve those objectives. If they do, then they need to determine how to organize the players on the field. If they do not, then the coaches need to invest in bringing in the necessary skills from outside. Once the season starts, making significant changes to the teams is difficult. The coaches will need to use their knowledge and leadership skills to guide their existing teams to success.

Once a company's structure and resources are aligned to its chosen strategy, the key question is whether the organization is focused enough to deliver the intended results. If the answer is no, chances are that the strategy will not be successfully executed. This will be discussed later, but successful strategy execution is not so much about how well the strategy is defined; instead, success depends on project selection, effective organizational alignment, relentless execution and focus.

Consequences of Being Unfocused

As explained in Chapter 3, top management's failure to effectively understand, control and manage the interdependencies between change-the-business and run-the-business activities results in a highly unfocused organization. When a company is highly unfocused, its employees are highly unfocused too. The consequences of being an unfocused organization are discussed below.

POORLY EXECUTED STRATEGY

According to the *Harvard Business Review*, over 90 per cent of strategies fail due to poor execution.[1] Being unfocused means that strategy objectives have not been clearly articulated or communicated to the entire organization. Often, there are too many objectives or, even worse, the objectives are not prioritized. Top management wants to do too many things and does not involve employees in the strategy formulation. Thus, employees neither understand nor buy into the long-term mission.

As mentioned earlier, being unfocused can mean that management fails to distinguish between run-the-business and change-the-business objectives.

---

1   See R. Kaplan and D. Norton (2001), *The Strategy-Focused Organization: How Balanced Scorecard Companies Thrive in the New Business Environment*.

Chapter 3 suggested that companies use 'change' to increase and create long-term value and 'run' to capture that value.

WEAK FINANCIAL PERFORMANCE

If the strategy is poorly executed, the financial objectives will be difficult to achieve. Unfocused companies typically generate significant costs over the years. They often run too many projects, not recognizing that projects are expensive and consume both financial and staff resources. In addition, they frequently lack a clear, transparent and objective project selection process (or investment committee). Investment decisions are made on partial information and the tendency is to start all projects whose business case 'looks good on paper.'

Finally, the overlap of change-the-business and run-the-business activities creates lots of waste, which translates into cost. Companies tend to be lean and cost-efficient with run-the-business activities; but if their change-the-business activities are not also lean the result can be very costly.

ORGANIZATIONAL OVERLAPS AND INTERNAL COMPETITION

When change-the-business and run-the-business activities are not clearly defined (and doing so is difficult), overlaps occur between several parts of the organization. Roles and responsibilities are unclear and projects compete against each other. In the end, people are not placed in those functions or projects where they perform best, which wastes lots of talent and energy in useless conflicts. As a result, internal competition surges and management focuses on politics and challenging their opponents. Career progression is reserved for those who wage the best contest rather than for those who deliver the best results. This internal strife creates a negative culture which impedes an execution culture.

LACK OF EXECUTION CULTURE

Without focus a company cannot achieve an execution culture. As mentioned previously, unfocused companies pursue too many objectives and have too many initiatives. During the workshops conducted with senior managers, I asked them to list their company's top three objectives. There was never unanimous agreement. If top management is not clear about the initiatives on which to focus the company's efforts, then staff will never know where to invest their time. As can be seen in Figure 4.1, the greater the number of strategic

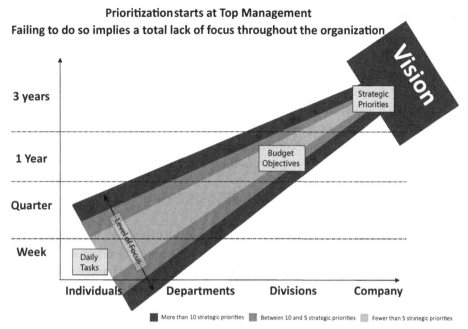

Figure 4.1   Consequences of a lack of priorities at the top of the
organization

objectives and priorities, the more unfocused are the employees. Alternatively,
the more focused is top management, the clearer employees and departments
are about what they need to do on a daily basis. When priorities cascade
down the organization, the result is often a distorted focus – and frequently
a significant distortion. The situation might be similar to that shown in red in
the chart.

Another significant consequence is that lack of focus leads to lack of
discipline in executing organizational objectives. Focus imposes discipline
because staff at any level know what to do at any point.

A final sign related to lack of focus and execution culture is when companies
brainstorm the same ideas again and again. Decisions are either not made or,
when they are made, they are continually refined before they are carried out.
I am not arguing against brainstorming; on the contrary, it is a positive way
to involve the entire organization in decision buy-in or in obtaining broader
points of views. But brainstorming a new initiative or overall strategy should
take no longer than a few weeks, after which management is responsible for
making decisions.

UNHAPPY, UNENGAGED AND UNMOTIVATED STAFF

One of the most dramatic consequences of being an unfocused company is the impact on staff. Lack of clear direction and priorities causes staff to be unhappy in what they do because they do not understand how their work contributes to the company's goals. Staff who are working on projects feel that management disregards their issues or achievements. They choose to work only the number of hours stipulated in their contracts. Or, even worse, they become regular absentees. Thus, unfocused companies do not get the most out of their staff.

UNBALANCED DISTRIBUTION OF RESOURCES

Management needs to decide every year how to distribute the company's limited resources, specifically its staff and financial assets. Decisions regarding how much and where to allocate resources are not easy. Management at an unfocused company often fails to regard these decisions as part of their key responsibilities because they lack clarity about the run-the-business/change-the-business dimensions. Consequently, the distribution of work within the business becomes totally unbalanced and grows out of control.

I have developed a matrix that illustrates this situation (Figure 4.2). The x-axis refers to the dimension of the business, either run-the-business or change-the-business. The y-axis represents both the front/core activities of the business and the support activities. For simplicity, I assume that most of the strategic growth projects are launched by the front side of the business – which is not too far from reality if we consider that research and development (R&D), business development, marketing and corporate are the departments that launch most of these growth initiatives – while the functions are more involved in cost-reduction projects (including performance improvement and system automation). Management has to make sure that the distribution of its resources is totally aligned and reflects the strategic objectives, in which case the chances are high that the strategy will be successful.

Figure 4.2 illustrates a well-balanced company whose resources are aligned to its strategic objectives. This company aims to increase its revenues and market share by expanding and establishing new shops. At the same time, the company wants to keep costs under control. The matrix shows that the company dedicates 75 per cent of its resources to run-the-business activities. In principle this can be a bit too much, considering that the modern trend is towards a 50/50 allocation; but the company is moving from an 80/20 situation.

DISTRIBUTION OF THE COMPANY RESOURCES AND ASSETS

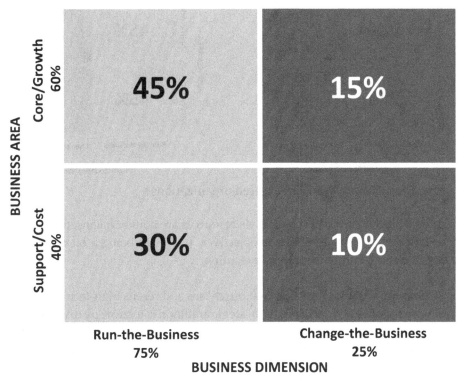

Figure 4.2   Resources distribution matrix

In terms of business activities, the company is slightly inclined towards growth due to the creation of new shops, which is in line with the strategic objectives. This company has the right settings to succeed in its strategy execution.

Conversely, Figure 4.3 shows examples of two companies that are unbalanced and thus become totally unfocused. Their management is not in control of these dimensions.

Company A is a multinational pharmaceutical business that aims to reduce its operating costs while growing by acquisition. It has allocated most of its resources to run-the-business activities, in particular on the front side. As a result of this allocation, the company has been able to create a strong sales and marketing force. Part of the back and support activities were outsourced five years ago, which is why this part of the business is provided with limited resources. In terms of change-the-business activities, the company is investing all allocated resources in R&D projects, looking for the new formula that will

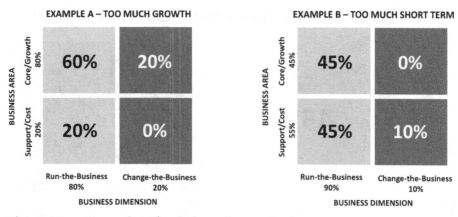

Figure 4.3   Examples of unbalanced organizations

become a blockbuster. This company's resources are neither balanced nor well distributed to achieve its strategic objectives, the result being a lack of focus that will cause a failure in strategy execution.

Company B is a local retailer that purchases and resells high-tech products through a number of franchises. Its strategic ambition is to grow by diversifying into new products and developing services related to the sale of its products. The distribution of resources is heavily oriented towards run-the-business activities, which is normal in such an industry. The few projects that the company is running are related to the installation of a new point-of-sale (POS) system and the development of training for new staff. This company will never achieve its strategy because its allocation of resources is neither optimal nor balanced.

MISMANAGED AND MISALIGNED PORTFOLIO OF PROJECTS

Another important consequence of being an unfocused organization is that management does not properly manage its portfolio of projects – i.e., the change-the-business dimension; nor are the projects aligned with the organization's strategy. There are two main related issues.

First, unfocused companies have too many projects. Chapter 3 discusses several reasons why projects proliferate if top management does not manage them proactively. Lack of focus causes most new projects to be categorized as 'high-priority,' which is made worse by the fact that most projects are not fully under management control. I have not come across any company that can provide on the spot a list of all its current projects, their business case, status, cost or time left to completion. For example, management at a mobile telecom provider told me recently that they had more than 300 projects running but they could not tell me the exact number. They did not know which were the top ten projects, the most strategic or the most important for the business. Most of these projects had been approved and launched with just an email rather than a thorough, detailed business case. Even more shocking was the fact for many projects it was not clear which department had requested the project (sponsor): 'In case of doubt, it is always our IT department that takes the lead,' they told me.

Because 30–40 per cent of company resources are spent on projects, not knowing their status, how they are performing or their expected returns is frightening. I also wonder why accountants do not look more seriously into this issue and why shareholders do not demand more discipline regarding project portfolio management.

Second, an unfocused organization's project investments are not reflective of the organization's strategy. As will be discussed later, the project portfolio should reflect the company's objectives not only to management but also to the entire organization. If this is not the case, it is usually due to the fact that projects have not been selected in a structured, top-down, efficient and disciplined manner – which is even more challenging when a company lacks full awareness of the projects it is running.

If the company has too many projects or the projects are not prioritized, employees will be unaware of the company's strategic objectives or how they should contribute to achieve them; and, worst of all, the strategy will not be properly executed.

Top management needs to learn to say 'no' to new projects as well as to ideas for new products/services. As Steve Jobs rightly pointed out, saying 'no' is one of the most important, but also one of the most difficult tasks of a leader.

Figure 4.4 illustrates an unbalanced portfolio of projects at a bank. Most of the projects are designed to achieve short-term growth. The bank has faced increased competition and is launching new products to try to recover lost market share. Most of these projects are very risky, for example, the attempt to integrate 15 retail branches recently acquired from a bank that went bankrupt. Since none of the projects will deliver benefits in the long term, how the bank will deliver sustainable growth is unclear. Finally, the bank is not running any

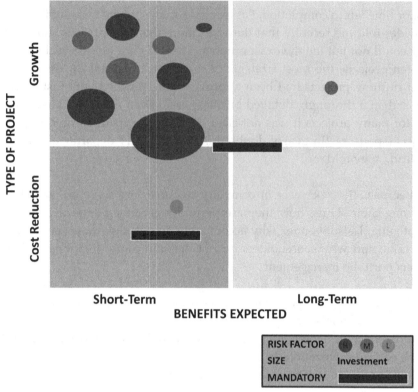

Figure 4.4   Example unbalanced portfolio

projects to reduce costs. This means that soon its cost/income ratio will increase, especially if the growth projects fail.

This figure illustrates many reasons why the bank will not achieve its strategy. I will explain later what a balanced and aligned portfolio in a focused organization looks like.

The Human Tendency to Be Unfocused

As mentioned in Chapter 3, human beings tend to be unfocused, with research by Gilbert and Killingsworth of Harvard showing that at any given time 50 per cent of the population is unfocused:[2] thus, half a company's staff are not focused on their work. Their study also showed that those people who were focused on their tasks were happier and performed up to 60 per cent more than

---

2   See Chapter 3, note 10.

those who were unfocused. Whatever people were doing, whether working or reading or shopping, they tended to be happier if they focused on the activity instead of thinking about something else. Successful people, such as Jack Welch or Steve Jobs, have been extremely focused.

According to the Harvard study, 30–40 per cent of employees' time in the workplace is spent dealing with unplanned interruptions and restoring the loss of mental focus they caused. This was not the case 20 years ago, simply because there were fewer tools of interruption. As stated earlier, this lack of focus leads not only to unhappiness but also to errors, wasted time, misunderstanding and, ultimately, to lower productivity and lost income.

THE NEED FOR DISCIPLINE AND ORDER

The fact is that nature tends towards disorder and that being focused requires discipline and order – so focus requires energy and effort. We humans have mixed feelings about expending energy, even if we know it will bring us pleasure. For example, in the Harvard study the second-highest rated activity in terms of providing happiness was physical exercise – and how many of us avoid that?

If top management does not 'encourage' its staff to focus, or does not even 'impose' focus, on key tasks and priorities, the chances are very high that employees' minds will wander during their working hours. They may work on those tasks they think are important, which are often the easier tasks; or respond to emails; or they may spend most of their time in meetings. Even worse, lack of focus can lead staff to waste time on the Internet or dealing with personal matters.

THE IMPACT ON PRODUCTIVITY

It is difficult to estimate the amount of waste that is created by unfocused companies and unfocused employees. To come up with a rough calculation, I took a simple measurement of labour productivity, such as the ratio of the real value of the company's labour output to its input (hours worked).[3] For the sake of simplicity, I excluded the qualitative aspects of labour productivity such as creativity, innovation, teamwork and improved quality of work. The following sample productivity calculation applies primarily to run-the-business activities:

---

3   See http://www.bls.gov/news.release/prin1.nr0.htm.

Units produced: 10,000

Standard price: €80/unit

Labour input: 1,000 hours

→ In a focused company the work is done in half of the time,
  thus 500 hours.

Cost of labour: €40/hour

Cost of material: €2,000

Cost of overhead: 2 × labour input

As can be seen in Figure 4.5, this simple example shows that an increase in staff focus directly affects the overall productivity of the company by increasing output, lowering production costs or even reducing prices – but remember that this type of increase in productivity applies mainly to run-the-business activities.

A. Unfocused Organization

$$\frac{10{,}000 \times 80}{1{,}000 \quad 40 + 10{,}000 + 80{,}000} = \frac{800{,}000}{130{,}000} = 6.15 \quad \text{productivity factor}$$

B. Focused Organization

$$\frac{10{,}000 \times 80}{500 \quad 40 + 10{,}000 + 40{,}000} = \frac{800{,}000}{70{,}000} = 11.43 \quad \text{productivity factor}$$

Figure 4.5   Productivity simulation

Improved focus on the change-the-business dimension will increase productivity by:

• Significantly decreasing the company's projects (cost reduction).

- Improving the selection of those projects that will bring the highest return to the business.

- Adjusting the organization to facilitate the execution of projects.

- Helping the allocation of the best people to the most strategic and important projects, which increases the probability of achieving results successfully and more quickly.

Why Being Focused Improves Strategy Implementation

Being focused improves the way organizations implement their strategy because the world is full of distractions, at levels much higher now than 20 or 30 years ago. Today, there is an overload of information, technology, products, services, telephones, emails and so forth. In addition, people seem to have personal lives that are busier than ever before. Our lives pass by quickly and we have too many things to do but not enough time to do them. Because employees are the most important component of an organization, the complexity of their lives affects the company as well.

The good thing about being focused is that it sets priorities and boundaries for both organizations and individuals. For example, a good friend of mine is a partner at PricewaterhouseCoopers (PwC), one of the big four audit firms. She prioritizes her work based on its importance to the firm. Often, she starts with client work. When she is focused on a task, her team knows that she cannot be interrupted. In meetings, she attends regularly, participates actively and is never distracted by activities such as glancing at her Blackberry. She is also very focused on her specialization, which has been Treasury since she began as an auditor with PwC more than 20 years ago. Because she has never changed her area of concentration, she has become one of Treasury's global thought leaders. She is able to concentrate all her energy on the topic in hand and keep her focus until the issue is resolved; as a result, she is very successful and happy.

The same applies to an organization. For example, when Steve Jobs returned to his old job at Apple in 1997 he decided that in order for the company to stay alive it had to focus on what it did best. He decided to concentrate all the company's energy on just four products – two laptops and two desktops – and to cancel all the other unrelated initiatives, projects and products. Steve Jobs' strong focus was transmitted to his team and in turn to the entire organization.

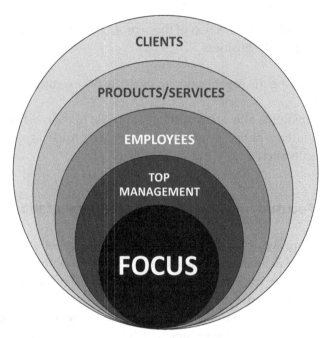

Figure 4.6   Focus reaches everywhere

In fact, I can make a strong statement based on my many years of observation: *Every business is focused when it is just starting up*. Those companies that manage to stay focused on their core and successfully complete the three steps discussed at the beginning of this chapter will likely succeed and stay in business. Those that do not stay focused will probably fail. The problems start when companies grow, at which point remaining focused becomes very difficult (for example, Apple when it became a public company and hired an external CEO). Management changes and new managers want to introduce new things, thus decreasing focus. The fascinating thing about achieving focus is that it affects the fundamental elements that make up an organization (Figure 4.6).

- **Top Management**. CEOs and top management have to regularly digest thousands of documents and deal with many gigabytes of information. Based on their ability to synthesize all of this information, they have to make critical decisions that affect the entire company as well as less critical decisions that can impact on parts of the organization. When CEOs or managers are focused they spend most of their time where they can add the most value.

  Focused managers also say no to initiatives that are not in line with the company's strategy and follow projects through until their benefits are delivered. Their focused approach is transmitted to their subordinates, which sets the right tone even if employees do not themselves become immediately focused. When CEOs are focused, the chances that their organizations will also be focused are much higher, as indicated in the Steve Jobs example.

- **Employees**. An average person's already limited attention span continues to diminish. In addition employees are often involved in too many projects, often combined with full-time jobs in the run-the-business dimension, and do not know which one to complete first. Thus, they focus on the easiest or most urgent tasks, leaving the difficult ones for later. These two factors –short attention span and overabundance of projects – dramatically affect staff productivity.

  In contrast, when top management is focused, employees become focused and are better able to work on the tasks that help their businesses achieve their strategic objectives. Focused employees get less distracted and often put in more work than required because, as we saw earlier, focused people are happier than unfocused people. They have a greater feeling of accomplishment, they become passionate about their work, they are ready to walk the extra mile, to stretch beyond their comfort zone and they look forward to going to the office.

- **Products/Services**. Focus also has a positive impact on the products and services that organizations produce and sell. Because focus means specialization and excellence, focused organizations tend to concentrate on a few products or services close to their core competencies that they excel at or that give them a competitive advantage, as Michael Porter would say.

  Specialization reduces the number of projects, products and services. By having fewer products, companies can increase their investment in more added-value activities, such as innovation, product quality, marketing or human resource (HR) development. In addition, because management considers only those ideas that seem really worthwhile, the number of new products diminishes and better ideas are generated. The result of Steve Jobs cutting the 30-plus products that Apple was selling in 1997 to four products are clear to everybody. This focus on a few products and core competencies helps companies execute their strategies.

- **Clients**. Finally, clients are more confident buying products and services from focused organizations because focus quickly builds a strong brand. Clients prefer to pay for those products or services where they feel they will receive value, particularly in a marketplace glutted with millions of products and brands. Knowing that a company is focused facilitates the purchasing decision; and if the clients have good experience, repeat purchases are virtually guaranteed.

A good example of how focus influences customers' purchases is the Mexican brewing company Grupo Modelo, producers of Corona Extra. Although the company sold a few brands besides Corona Extra, its management's primary focus was on the marketing, quality, investment in and international expansion of this particular product. The result was that in 1989 Corona was introduced and quickly became the second best-selling imported light beer and the first beer to sell more than 1 million cases in its introductory year. Today, Corona is one of the five top-selling beers worldwide. Thus, focus also facilitates the way in which companies implement their strategies, as sales growth is always one of the recurring elements of every strategy.

My thesis is that if all of the organization's fundamental elements benefit from becoming focused, the chances of improving strategy implementation are very high. As we will see later though, a focused organization is not guaranteed to become a successful company. Although becoming focused will increase the chances of successful strategy execution, the strategy chosen and the decisions made must be the right ones.

The Characteristics of a Focused Organization

A company's successful strategy execution depends not only on whether the company performs well. A successful company also:

- Achieves sustainable growth of both revenues and profits.

- Consistently delivers its strategy.

- Outperforms the competition.

- Is viewed as a market leader.

- Has fulfilled staff.

Market value is also very important, although I believe that successful strategy implementation is not the only factor that determines a company's share price. Other influences include the overall state of the economy or stock market fluctuations. Nevertheless, I believe that if a company consistently executes and delivers its strategy, over time it will rise above its direct competitors.

One of the outcomes of my research was that the most successful organizations were not just reaching but were also exceeding their strategic objectives. Although having a great leader, a well-known brand and a very good product or service contributed to this success, what made all the difference in their ability to surpass their expectations was the fact that they were FOCUSED.

To better explain the key elements a company needs to be successful in their strategy execution, I turned the word FOCUSED into an acronym.

- **F – Fewer projects**, rather than many. A focused organization that is able to effectively select and prioritize its projects and invest in just three to five good initiatives at a time clearly outperforms organizations that take on too many projects. The few projects that are selected are linked to one or several strategic objectives and are fully supported by top management.

  Top management monitors the execution of these strategic projects at least monthly and closely follows through until the projects are completed and the benefits delivered. It is essential that these few initiatives be communicated and understood by the entire organization.

  The chance of having the organization understand and remember three initiatives is higher than if the company were faced with multiple initiatives. Also, because only three to five strategic projects are selected each year, management is forced to find the best ideas.

  The maximum numbers of projects, by strategic ranking, that a company should expect to execute successfully are two AAA, one

AA or one A (see the classifications in Table 1.2). Strategic projects require full management attention; therefore carrying out more than three almost guarantees failure.

- **O – Organized staff.** A focused enterprise is made out of the very best professionals and only the best survive. The staff is organized in such a way that all personnel know what is expected of them. They do not waste time on activities that are not part of their core skill set; rather, they focus on their key strengths and core capabilities instead of continually trying to improve their weaknesses.

  Run-the-business activities are clearly differentiated from change-the-business activities, and the latter's resources are identified. Project managers, project leaders, programme managers and people working in programme management offices manage the day-to-day 'change' activities, with the input and collaboration of the run-the-business resources. Some of these resources will occasionally work full time for the change-the-business, with management making the decisions and setting the priorities. One big difference is that the key initiatives are staffed with the best people.

  Top management has also to split their time between change and run managerial activities and participate as project sponsors, on project steering committees and dealing with such day-to-day operational activities as sales meetings. Because they have set the business's priorities, they know how to distribute their time most effectively.

- **C – Competitive mindset.** The focused company competes with the outside world rather than internally, using innovation and excellence as its main differentiation. Internal competition, which is so negative in the long term, is eliminated because all of the organization's effort is placed on doing what it does best in order to beat the competition. The CEO and top management explicitly identify rival organizations, often referring to them in their speeches and communications to the company.

  The focused company is also very clear about how to beat the competition. In fact, there is only one way: creating better products/

delivering better services. A high degree of *innovation* is a key and common characteristic of a focused organization.

In addition, the employees of such companies tend to have winning attitudes. They are talented and ambitious and want to progress in their careers. Unlike employees in unfocused organizations, they do not compete with their fellow employees because the focus on outside forces is so strong. Examples of this external competition exist in almost every industry: Windows vs Mac, Google vs Yahoo, Facebook vs LinkedIn, Shell vs BP, HP vs Dell, Boeing vs Airbus, and many more. Companies that operate in different industries can have several competitors at the same time; for example Microsoft competes with both Apple and Google.

• **U – Urgency.** In business, time is money – even more so with the current level of globalization. Organizations need to launch their initiatives quickly. The time to market for new products must become shorter and shorter. Creating a sense of urgency is a competitive advantage, and the focused organization is always aware of this fact. Urgency is also needed to focus staff and encourage them to give their best performance. Ensuring that employees are very familiar with the key strategic projects selected by top management helps to build this sense of urgency. Employees know that they cannot postpone their work and that they have to deliver on time what is expected from them.

Clear deadlines, fixed goals and knowledge of the importance (and benefits) of each strategic project are tools with which to infuse the entire organization, both management and staff, with urgency and focus. These techniques also provide the sense that things are moving faster, almost as if the tempo at which the company usually works is doubled or tripled. People work harder, the tempo seems faster and results are achieved more quickly. This sense of urgency can be achieved in both the run-the-business and change-the-business dimensions. However, pressure can be applied more strongly to the change-the-business side, which would then serve as a driver for activities in the rest of the organization.

One point to take into account – and a *real warning* for top management – is to impose the sense of urgency carefully. If management and staff are pushed too hard for too long, they will not be able to cope with the pace and will burn out. A collateral issue is that when pushed too hard to perform, people tend to take higher risks than normal. At first, this behaviour may pay off; but in the long term, it is not sustainable. In addition, management and staff may find ways to produce exceptional results without following the 'rules.' Both scenarios often have disastrous consequences for organizations (see box below).

This is probably the *most important risk of a focused organization*. Putting too much pressure, for too long on the staff and the organization, what I refer to as *aggressive focus*, can bring amazing short-term results but in the long term is not sustainable.

- **S – Strategic alignment.** In a focused organization all staff are aware of the strategic objectives of the company and how they will be achieved. Every initiative in a focused organization's change-the-business dimension should be linked to one or several strategic objectives. Any initiative that is not so linked should be immediately cancelled. This alignment is necessary to ensure that the company achieves its stated goals. All departments work in an integrated

---

In 2005, a new CEO arrived at one of Belgium's leading banks with a mission to grow the bank internationally and bring it into the European Ivy League of banks. He created focus by setting two clear targets: to increase the benefit per share by at least 10 per cent between 2005 and 2009; to double the profit coming from outside Benelux, from 15 per cent in 2004 to 30 per cent. He also introduced a few strategic initiatives that would help achieve these targets. Beginning with his management team, the new CEO quickly increased the focus and pressure in the entire organization.

This approach worked for three years, with the organization moving faster and faster and targets being met. One of the CEO's strategic initiatives was to buy a small bank in the US to build and sell in the subprime market. At the same time, an opportunity arose to join a consortium of leading banks, Royal Bank of Scotland and Banco Santander, in buying one of the leading banks in the world, the Dutch ABN AMRO.

With two highly strategic projects immediately following a couple of years of aggressive focus and pressure, management and most of the staff were exhausted. The organization could not cope and, with the collapse of the financial market, went into bankruptcy.

manner towards achieving those objectives, removing any room for a creation of silos.

Having only a few key projects is the best contribution to strategy achievement. For example, recently a consumer goods producer decided to acquire a company in China that built and sold ironing machines. This project was perfectly aligned with the company's strategy, which was to have a presence in China and to increase profits coming from that region by 20 per cent. The company successfully acquired and integrated the Chinese plant, which immediately provided a 30 per cent profit coming from the Asian region.

- **E – Excellence.** A focused organization applies the highest standards to everything it does, and its products and/or services are known for their quality. Sustainable excellence requires attention to the details of every aspect of the organization: values, quality of employees, internal and external processes, products, and customer service.

  A focused organization is a place where imagination is nurtured, applied and executed while ensuring excellence in all that it does. Employees understand the importance of quality and continuous improvement. They also know that there is no compromise on quality and they should strive towards perfection, which stretches staff beyond their limits.

  The key strategic initiatives are managed and staffed by the most capable people. Both the project sponsor and the project team are selected according to which employees throughout the organization will be the best at driving the initiative. This approach leaves little room for internal politics.

- **D – Discipline.** Companies today need discipline to execute their strategy and key initiatives; without it, consistent performance becomes very difficult. Discipline can be defined as '*training to act in accordance with rules*' or '*the activity, exercise, or regimen that develops or improves a skill.*' It requires practice and helps organizations react quickly and perform efficiently. One of the most disciplined organizations, the army, would not be able to carry out its defence programmes without discipline

Discipline should not be seen as something negative that inhibits innovation. Rather, innovation depends on discipline. Companies should clearly distinguish between time set aside for creativity and time allocated to strategy execution. Focused organizations are able to make this distinction and move from the creative phase to the execution phase very quickly. If companies spend too much on innovation, they will be too late by the time they decide to execute their strategy. The challenge for the CEO and the company's entire management team is to find the right balance between discipline and creativity/flexibility.

Discipline for the staff means that once the strategic project has been approved by top management, it should be meticulously executed without being questioned again and again. This does not mean that there is no room for discussion, especially if the project faces unexpected issues during the design or implementation phase; but the project selection should not be further debated.

One final and very important aspect of discipline in a focused organization is that required by the CEO and top management when waiting to see results. Many of the benefits of strategic initiatives are not seen until the medium to long term, and management must be patient to achieve the bigger results. Too much emphasis on short-term results will eventually be harmful.

The Benefits of Becoming a Focused Organization

The benefits of becoming a focused organization are significant, with the most important outlined below.

ACHIEVE STRATEGIC GOALS

Everybody in the focused organization, from the CEO to the accounts payable employee, knows the direction in which the organization is going; which two to three initiatives are the most important for that year; and the business case for these few critical initiatives.

Both the run-the-business and the change-the-business dimensions have clear objectives that are well defined. All the friction and overlaps between these two dimensions are removed, and both sides are perfectly aligned and support each other to achieve their respective objectives. While the run-the-business objectives pertain primarily to sales and operations, the change-the-business focus is on longer-term targets. Because its key initiatives are selected using objective and transparent methods, because their business case is well understood and because management follows up on the initiatives until they are completed and the benefits are achieved, the focused organization is the ideal model for executing the company's strategy.

ATTAIN FINANCIAL RESULTS

Positive financial results are a direct consequence of achieving the company's strategy. In the end it is probably the most important benefit of becoming a focused organization, since organizations need to have good financial results to survive and provide a good return to their shareholders.

The benefits of becoming focused can be significant and the results can appear very quickly on the company's bottom line, particularly on the cost side. Costs are reduced when irrelevant projects are cancelled, which can add up to huge savings. Between 10 and 20 per cent of projects could be easily cancelled without any major impact, which in turn frees up budgets and resources to execute key strategic projects. In addition, the number of consultants who either manage or staff these projects will be significantly decreased, as will the fees paid to them. Finally, because the focused organization chooses primarily those initiatives that will maximize the company's value creation, and management pushes the organization to execute them, top-line benefits can also be significant.

BECOME A HIGH-PERFORMING ORGANIZATION

Because a focused organization is clearly organized, assigns its employees to positions best suited to them and clearly defines it goals, it becomes a high-performing organization. It is not just a team that is high performing, which can be the case in a very strategic project; it is the entire organization. The run-the-business personnel want to produce and deliver the best product to the customers, while the change-the-business employees want to select and execute the highest-added-value projects.

A high-performing team is characterized by a magic feeling among its members. A team of people can achieve a sum far greater than the sum of their individual skills alone. As Katzenbach and Smith describe it: 'A high performing team is a small number of people with complementary skills who are committed to a common purpose, performance goals, and approach for which they hold themselves mutually accountable.'[4]

In my experience a high-performing team is rare but when it occurs, all members give their best, work hard, are committed, do not engage in internal competition and are happy and feel proud to belong to that team. The same is true of a focused – high-performing – organization: employees are happy to work there, are very strongly committed and are proud to show that they work for such a good company. Obviously, all these smaller benefits turn into large benefits for the organization: successful strategy execution and improved financial results.

DEVELOP A WINNING CULTURE OF GETTING THINGS DONE

Today, many organizations enjoy discussing new business initiatives, especially in lengthy meetings; but they stop at the discussion stage. Alternately, companies start initiatives and after a few months resume arguing about decisions made in the past. Progress is very slow and the initiatives' momentum is stifled.

A focused organization selects just a few initiatives and gets them done before starting new ones. Once an initiative has been chosen, all the company's focus is on execution. Results are shown in short time frames and progress is monitored according to plan. Building momentum is very important when creating a culture of getting things done, and the CEO and top management need to lead by example.

BUILD A HAPPY, COMMITTED AND ENGAGED WORKFORCE

The last major benefit of a focused organization is that its employees are satisfied and have a positive sense of accomplishment. They work in the position they are best at and which adds the most value to the organization; and they like what they do, as opposed to just performing a job. As mentioned here and, shown in Figure 4.7, focusing on these three areas and spending most of the time in the intersection brings not only the highest level of

---

4   J. Katzenbach and D. Smith (2003), *The Wisdom of Teams: Creating the High-Performance Organization*, 45.

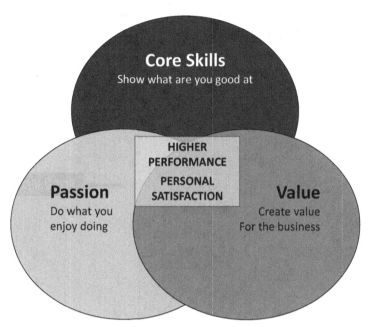

Figure 4.7   Where to focus?

satisfaction to each individual but also the highest level of performance from each individual.

One Example That Works: Apple, Inc.

Apple, Inc. is probably the best example of what I consider to be a focused organization. The company was founded by Steve Jobs and Steve Wozniak in April 1976 in a garage in Santa Clara, California.[5] Between 1978 and 1980, sales grew from $7.8 million to $117 million. After losing a power struggle with the board of directors in 1985, Jobs resigned from Apple. Some wrong decisions and several years of decreasing sales put Apple on the verge of bankruptcy.

In 1997 Steve Jobs was called back to lead the company he had founded 20 years earlier. Upon his return, Jobs transformed Apple into a focused organization. The results have been reflected in the company's stock price, which can be seen in Figure 4.8. In order to transform Apple into a focused organization, Steve Jobs made a number of changes, as outlined on the following page.

---

5   Leander Kahney (2009), *Inside Steve's Brain: Business Lessons from Steve Jobs, the Man who Saved Apple.*

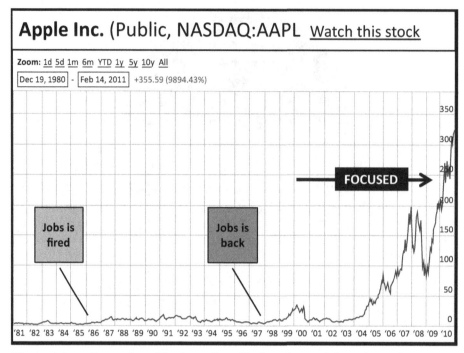

Figure 4.8   Example – The benefits of being focused (Apple Inc.)

Fewer Projects	Jobs cancelled nearly 300 projects – from almost all of the hardware, including prototype computers, to new software – and laid off thousands of workers. He simplified the products pipeline from about 40 different machines to four: two notebooks and two desktops in two markets – consumer and professional. *'We've got to focus and do things we can be good at – only way to save the company.'*[6]
Organized Staff	Based on his view that the quality of Apple's staff was a competitive advantage, Jobs eliminated the weakest performers and kept only the most talented people. He insisted that staff work on what they are best at and his project teams were staffed only with high-calibre personnel. *'We can put our A team on every single project instead of having a B or C team.'*
Competitive Mindset	Dell, Microsoft, Google and Sony are Apple's well-known competitors. Steve Jobs had a very competitive mindset, which he transmitted to the entire organization. His method of competing with these companies was through true innovation: developing better products, better services and better customer experience. This competitive mindset is evident in some of Apple's advertisements, which can seem sarcastic about the competition.[7] *'We beat Dell on operational metrics every quarter.'*[8]

6   Kahney, *Inside Steve's Brain*, 25.
7   Kahney, *Inside Steve's Brain*, 36. In August 1981 IBM released their PC. Unimpressed and unafraid, Apple welcomed IBM to the PC market with a slightly smug full-page ad in the *Wall Street Journal* – 'Welcome, IBM. Seriously.'
8   Steve Jobs: The *Rolling Stone* Interview, 4 April 1996.

Urgency	When Jobs came back to Apple in 1997, he noticed that the company and its employees were very laid-back. Together with instilling some discipline, Jobs renewed the sense of urgency in the company. One method he used was to establish the biannual Apple Worldwide Developers Conference, where new Apple products are officially released. Failure to meet the deadlines for this conference is not an option, and everyone at Apple knows this. This kind of urgency creates focus and can really drive productivity.
Strategic Alignment	Apple's strategic goals are not explicitly stated. However, one message that is clearly communicated is that industry leadership requires that Apple's products be differentiated from those of the competition in terms of function, design and brand image. This differentiation gives Apple a competitive advantage in an environment in which trends and technology change rapidly. People value uniqueness, and every aspect of Apple, Inc. is aligned with this goal. The few projects that Apple launches every year are fully aligned with its ambition to innovate, differentiate and excel.
Excellence	Steve Jobs pursuit of excellence is one of the secrets of Apple's great design. Apple's products are developed through endless iterative processes of testing and prototypes. Everyone is included in the process, not just designers. Every detailed is discussed and thought out, with a big emphasis on simplification as the project evolves. Excellence at Apple is applied not only to the product design but also to the product launch. For example, Jobs wanted the product's presentation to the public to be faultless. He checked that everything was perfect, including how the light reflected on the product. *'Be a yardstick of quality. Some people aren't used to an environment where excellence is expected.'*
Discipline	Before Steve Jobs returned to Apple, employees arrived late and left early. Jobs imposed rigour, discipline and new rules. He was exceedingly demanding of the people who reported to him. Apple's middle management expects the same level of high performance from their staff. There is a constant tension at Apple between the fear of getting fired and a messianic zeal for making a dent in the universe. But even though working at Apple is demanding and stressful, all the staff love their jobs and are extremely loyal to the company – as they were to Steve Jobs. But here discipline extends beyond staff motivation or internal processes. For example Apple is extremely disciplined about pricing. The company sets the prices and keeps them the same in every store in every country. This pricing discipline enforces the brand and the image of excellence.

Apple is a clear example of a focused organization, and the benefits are self-explanatory and evident to everyone. In the next chapters I will explain the practical steps for achieving a focused organization.

5

A Six-Pillar Framework for Becoming a Focused Organization

Becoming a focused organization requires a radical change in every single key element that composes a company. I have developed an easy-to-use framework that addresses these six critical pillars (Figure 5.1). This framework is based on a maturity model which specifies the steps that a company needs to go through to become focused. Most maturity models, such as the Capability Maturity Model

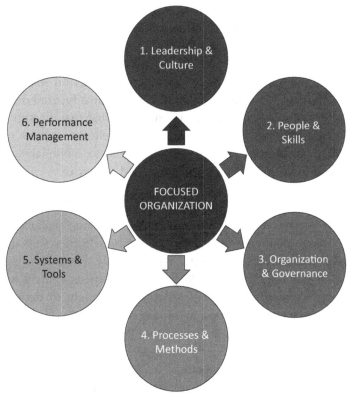

Figure 5.1   Six-pillar framework

Integration (CMMI) or the Organizational Project Management Maturity Model (OPM3), have five phases and can take between five and ten years to reach the highest level. The model that I propose, the Focused Maturity Model (FMM), has only two stages and can be fully implemented in less than 12 months.

Leadership and Culture

Leadership is where everything starts and ends in a company. Although a company's culture and values are defined over time and can remain unchanged for decades, the chief executive officer (CEO) and top management can alter these elements at any point with their messages and actions. In a focused organization the CEO is the main driver of change, thus he or she needs to be the first to adopt the culture and values and to gain top management's support in transmitting these principles to the rest of the organization.

Changes to a company's culture and values in order to create a focused organization can involve either incorporating new elements into the existing culture or replacing ones that no longer apply. The five focused values that pertain to leadership and culture outlined below.

- **Passion for excellence**. This is the first and most important value of all. If management is content producing and selling mediocre products, the company will never become a focused organization. This does not mean that a company must manufacture high-end products; rather, the passion for excellence applies equally to companies making low-cost products, to white-label producers and to businesses providing any kind of service.

- **True team spirit**. This value is essential in order for the company to become focused. Although most companies include teamwork as one of their core values, in reality self-interested individuals climb the corporate ladder more quickly, while team players are left behind. Often, this lack of team spirit is evident among top management, where fierce battles are fought to determine who keeps most of the power. Management's attitude then triggers a similar selfish attitude throughout the organization.

  In a focused organization, teamwork begins with the CEO and top management and is applied on a daily basis. Genuine team players are rewarded and promoted to higher positions in the organization, while self-interested personalities leave the company because they fail to find their place.

• **Cultivation of a creative environment**. Creativity should be fostered in every corner of the company, with each employee feeling free to propose ideas for new products or improvements in the way the company operates and services its customers. Run-the-business staff will often suggest product innovations, but these suggestions must be seamlessly integrated with the change-the-business side in order to be developed and brought to the market. Thus, creativity should be fostered on both sides of the business.

   Innovation need not always be linked to a new product; it can also involve improvements to existing products. A fair and transparent process should be used to select those ideas that will be implemented.

• **Relentless execution**. The focus on relentless execution is an uncommon value in today's organizations. Execution-centric companies are disciplined to systematically deliver until completion the few strategic initiatives chosen by top management. Such companies concentrate on activities that deliver the greatest benefit; confront and solve problems right away; are action-oriented and results driven; and are consistently faster to market than their competitors.

• **Dedication to fostering realized/fulfilled employees**. A focused organization is committed to fostering fulfilled employees by enabling them to concentrate on those activities in which they add the most value to the company. Despite the hard work involved, employees who are allowed to perform those tasks at which they excel generally achieve personal satisfaction and are happy about their workplace.

Focused Organization = Change-the-Business + Run-the-Business

Top management needs to be aware of how run-the-business and change-the-business activities operate independently and how they interact. In terms of leadership and culture, however, the five focused values discussed above apply to both dimensions.

People and Skills

It has been said repeatedly by many leaders and management gurus that people are the most important assets companies have. I strongly believe that this is true; but in a focused organization they must be *good* people: motivated and engaged, technical and expert, and led by good managers.

The People and Skills pillar comprises four important human resources categories which are carried out differently in change-the-business versus run-the-business dimensions:

- Competencies and talents.

- Training and development.

- Career path.

- Reward methods.

Although all four of these areas have seen improvements over the years, they are still focused primarily on the company's run-the-business side. When looking at how companies operate today in these areas, there is still a strong 'smell' of the old operations.

RUN-THE-BUSINESS

Because these four human resources categories almost fully centre on the run-the-business dimension, companies aiming to become focused do not need to change what already works. On the other hand, companies will need to adjust all four of these elements to enable the run-the-business and the change-the-business dimensions to interact seamlessly – which, as previously discussed, is the goal.

CHANGE-THE-BUSINESS

Because the People and Skills pillar is heavily oriented towards the run-the-business side of the company, it requires significant change in order to support change-the-business activities. The main elements that need to be adapted are detailed in the following pages.

Competencies and Skills

Change-the-business competencies are different from the competencies required to run the business. Project managers in both business dimensions theoretically should produce the same results: deliverables that meet sponsors' and stakeholders' expectations. However, project success depends on the context in which it is carried out and some projects are inherently harder to manage than others. To achieve a level of harmonious performance, a company needs to establish a competency model that manages and supports employees working on projects. This model is usually linked to a certification, at least for those employees who are dedicated full time to project management. Competencies for programme managers are slightly different than for project managers, but they are part of the natural evolution of a proficient project manager. On the other hand, competencies for project portfolio managers and chief strategy execution officers are much more business oriented and much less about project management.

Training and Development

Training must include a complete development programme specific to the change-the-business dimension and this programme should be linked directly to the competency model.

Many large organizations have limited in-house or external training for soon-to-be project managers and project team members. However, a comprehensive change-the-business training programme addresses not only these employees but also the CEO, top management and the rest of the management team. Management might not be trained in the technical aspects of project management but should understand the importance of projects, programmes and project portfolio management (PPM) to executing company strategy. The change-the-business training programme should be directly linked to the competency model.

Career Path

Career path refers to a planned progression of positions within specific professions (e.g., marketing and finance) through which employees can advance within the company. In most organizations today, career paths are well defined for the run-the-business side. For example, employees who begin their careers in sales follow a predetermined process that offers them more responsibilities every set number of years if they perform well. At a certain point, these high performers will begin to manage a group of people, a small department and will then become sales directors. Of course, this process depends on a number of variables, but at least the path has been defined.

Companies have defined a career path for project managers as well, but it is essentially artificial. The standard project manager career path includes the following levels:

1.　Project analyst (or team member).

2.　Project manager.

3.　Programme manager.

4.　Programme director.

A real career path for change-the-business should include additional steps, such as head of the programme management office (PMO), or project portfolio manager. It is particularly important for the career path to include time spent on the run-the-business side as well as the opportunity to ultimately become the organization's CEO.

Reward Methods

Staff working in the change-the-business dimension should be rewarded if strategic projects are executed well and results are achieved; however, most companies today reward their staff on only run-the-business achievements. Bonuses should be linked to project delivery, not only to business results, and a proportion of the rewards should be dedicated to change-the-business performance, including that of top management.

In addition, many companies pay projects managers less than professionals in such areas as client facing, finance or marketing. This discrepancy should be corrected.

Focused Organization = Change-the-Business + Run-the-Business

The biggest challenge to the People and Skills pillar of a focused organization is to seamlessly align two different sets of HR models. The organization must first define the change-the-business aspect and then integrate it fully with the run-the-business model. Highly motivated employees will gain experience in both dimensions, for example, spending two years in a marketing position and then moving on to manage a customer relationship management (CRM) implementation project. Employees cannot become managers if they have not previously managed a large project. It is important that HR management is aware of these different models and takes them into account when defining the organization's HR policies.

Organization and Governance

Having the right organizational and governing structure is probably the biggest challenge to becoming focused. Making changes within an organization is extremely complicated for two fundamental reasons: historical acumen and human behaviour. First, organizations are built over many years and over time they become rusty, expensive to run and out of touch with reality. Second, the hundreds and sometimes thousands of individuals that make up an organization have habits which they are often reluctant to change. Some of these individuals are also influenced by decision-making power, which is often reflected by who has the largest department, the highest budgets and the biggest salary.

Yet the market evolves, faster in some industries than others, and therefore companies have to constantly adapt their organizational structure. As explained in previous chapters, the growth of the change-the-business versus the run-the-business dimension has a huge impact. A focused organization needs to find the right balance between these two dimensions, which can be referred to as 'organizational alignment.' In a nutshell, the main difference between the two dimensions is that run-the-business is an activity that has to be carried out vertically (within departments), while change-the-business has to be carried out transversally or horizontally (across departments).

RUN-THE-BUSINESS

In terms of the Organization and Governance pillar, the run-the-business dimension is well established. In fact, this dimension is as solid as stone and difficult to modify.

To become focused, however, a company has to balance its resources, budgets and power between the run-the-business and change-the-business

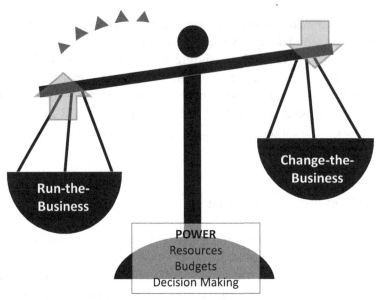

Figure 5.2   Organization power balance

components (Figure 5.2) – which is easier said than done. To begin with, the quest for power is deeply rooted in human nature. As explained earlier, it is often a zero sum process: what you add to one dimension you have to subtract from the other one. This calculation has an immediate impact on the side from which something is subtracted, and probably affects the entire business. Even if it is in the company's best interests, very few managers will voluntarily give power away to another manager by virtue of moving some of their resources or budgets to the change-the-business side. Either the incentives to make this happen must be strong or the CEO and top management need to exert extreme pressure.

CHANGE-THE-BUSINESS

This dimension is the one that has to change the most in terms of organization and governance. Although many organizations have undertaken a variety of measures – such as establishing PMOs or project support offices (PSOs) – to cope with the increase in projects, the implementation of these measures has not been very successful. Recent studies show that in 2007 three out of four PMOs closed after three years of going live, the main reason being that their value was not recognized and they were seen solely as an expense.[1] Companies

---

1   PM Solutions, *The State of the PMO*, available at http://www.pmsolutions.com/collateral/research/State%20of%20the%20PMO%202010%20Research%20Report.pdf.

Optimal Organizational Structure

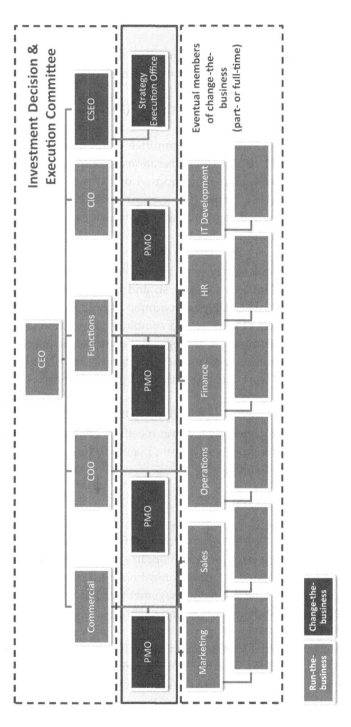

Figure 5.3 Example balanced organization

failed to understand how their change-the-business and run-the-business dimensions could be linked.

Adjusting the change-the-business dimension requires establishing an organizational structure such as that shown in Figure 5.3.

Investment Decision and Execution Committee (IDEC)

The investment decision and execution committee is composed of C-suites and is chaired by the CEO or the chief operations officer (COO). In large organizations, the committee could be composed of n-1 managers, as often they are more aware of the daily details. It is very important that the committee be neither managed nor chaired by the chief information officer (CIO) or IT director to avoid the risk of lack of buy-in.

The IDEC prioritizes and selects new investment proposals; ultimately decides in which projects/initiatives to invest; and determines the strategic roadmap for the company. The strategic roadmap should be composed of 20–30 projects, listed in order of priority and combining short- and long-term initiatives that reflect the company's strategy. For example, if international growth is one of the firm's main objectives, then the highest rank of the strategic roadmap should include at least one international expansion project.

Once the strategic roadmap is approved, the IDEC monitors its progress and execution in subsequent meetings. These meetings should take place at least once per quarter, preferably every month, mainly to put pressure on the organization to execute the roadmap.

Strategy Execution Office (SEO)

The main responsibility of the strategy execution office is the close follow-up of the implementation of the strategic roadmap. In addition, the SEO collects ideas for new projects generated by the organization's different departments, manages the network of programme management offices, arranges IDEC sessions and produces monthly execution status reports.

The SEO is led by the chief strategy execution officer (CSEO), who reports directly to the CEO and the IDEC – both of which monitor the strategic roadmap execution – and who is closely linked to the strategic planning office. In small companies, merging the strategic planning and the strategy execution offices is preferable. In large companies, keeping them separate is best because then the strategic planning office can focus on analysing markets and competition and defining company strategy. Both departments should interact but keep their independence.

An important feature of the SEO is the participation of a few very experienced project managers to execute some of the strategic projects, mainly those that touch all or most of the company's departments. Because these projects can be highly political and can require someone neutral to lead them, the SEO is able to play a critical role similar to a small internal consulting group within the organization. It is imperative that the members of the SEO know about both the content of the projects and how they link with the company's strategy.

Programme Management Office (PMO)

Each major department in the organization should establish its own PMO to support the projects executed in its business unit. All the PMOs should be linked, should apply the same processes and should use the same tools. It is very important that the project managers belong to one PMO (similar to the SEO). If not, PMOs will be considered as overhead and bureaucratic, which devalues the perception of project management and ultimately kills the transformation to a focused organization.

Project Support Office (PSO)

A project support office deals with a large strategic project's back office and administrative tasks. The PSO's added value is not visible, but some of the tasks it performs are essential to the successful execution of a strategic project. Typically, a PSO's responsibilities include time tracking, document management, issue management, risk management and keeping the project plan up to date. PSOs also make sure that company standards, processes and tools are correctly applied in the project.

Small projects should not have a PSO because these offices are costly and can slow down the project by creating too much red tape and paperwork.

Community of Project Managers

Because no single person is given ultimate responsibility for the change-the-business dimension, and because most of an organization's people and project managers are embedded in the run-the-business side, it is important to establish a strong community of project managers. The SEO should motivate and oversee the change-the-business community and should hold regular scheduled meetings, ideally once per quarter. This community is a transversal platform for exchanging lessons learned and discussing change-the-business issues pertaining to strategy execution.

Resource Management Committee

The main purpose of the resource management committee is to administer and foster the critical resources of the business. This committee should be supervised by the top level of the company, and the difficulty of its tasks should not be underestimated. Having a clear overview of how many resources are already committed to a project and how many resources are available is vital. The related skills and competencies also need to be identified and analysed. Although the committee's focus is primarily change-the-business resources, the business often needs a good overview of all of its resources.

I am often asked whether only one person should be in charge of the change-the-business dimension, but the nature of change-the-business activities and the impossibility of clearly separating them from the run-the-business side make this very difficult. Too many power struggles and conflicts would result. My recommendation is to establish a companywide committee, composed of all the top executives, that is responsible not only for the change-the-business activities but also for ensuring that they are effectively aligned with the run-the-business dimension. The CEO has ultimate responsibility for the company's change-the-business component but also oversees the run-the-business dimension. The SEO is responsible for day-to-day follow-up but has no decision-making powers.

Focused Organization = Change-the-Business + Run-the-Business

The Organization and Governance pillar is one of the most difficult business elements for which to find the right balance because both the organization and the external environment constantly change. Implementing the right connections between change-the-business and run-the-business activities is fundamental for the execution of the strategy. If this optimal balance is achieved, the organization will become extremely responsive to the changing environment and able to quickly react to the competition. Eventually, the organization can become a trendsetter in its industry.

Processes and Methods

Processes, methods and standards are necessary to ensure that work is performed consistently throughout the organization. Each process has a specific objective which requires the performance of certain activities to produce the desired output. Not only do processes help gauge performance and increase efficiency, they also facilitate continuous improvements and give management better control over the company.

Processes are traditionally divided into three categories – management processes, operating processes and supporting processes – all of which are oriented primarily toward run-the-business activities.

RUN-THE-BUSINESS

As presented in Chapter 1, Porter's value chain is a very good example of how business processes traditionally have been oriented towards the run-the-business dimension. Each department in today's run-the-business organization has its own processes, which are often linked to those that are corporate wide, and each of these processes is overseen by a process owner who is responsible for its correct implementation and follow-up.

Companies have developed process management systems, initiatives often led by the quality management department with the aim of achieving one of the many international quality certifications – such as International Organization for Standardization (ISO)[2] or Capability Maturity Model Integration (CMMI),[3] which pertains primarily to IT processes. But the ultimate goal of processes is to optimize the way work is performed, either by removing a non-added-value task, redesigning a task or automating parts of a task.

These efficiency improvements have historically focused on businesses' run-the-business dimension, which explains both why the room for improvement of this dimension is very limited and why the ruthless trend described in Chapter 1 is accelerated. Nevertheless, most organizations have mature run-the-business processes. This is not the case for the change-the-business dimension, whose processes are not fully developed and less embedded in the organization, or for the link between the two dimensions.

---

2   See http://www.iso.org/iso/home.html.
3   See http://www.sei.cmu.edu/cmmi.

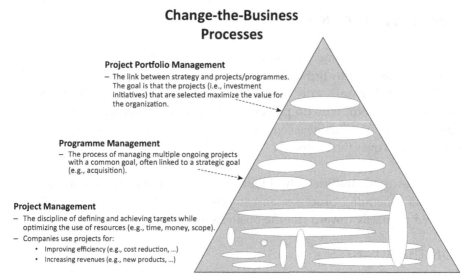

Change-the-Business Processes

Project Portfolio Management
- The link between strategy and projects/programmes. The goal is that the projects (i.e., investment initiatives) that are selected maximize the value for the organization.

Programme Management
- The process of managing multiple ongoing projects with a common goal, often linked to a strategic goal (e.g., acquisition).

Project Management
- The discipline of defining and achieving targets while optimizing the use of resources (e.g., time, money, scope).
- Companies use projects for:
  - Improving efficiency (e.g., cost reduction, ...)
  - Increasing revenues (e.g., new products, ...)

Figure 5.4   Project management-related processes

CHANGE-THE-BUSINESS

The goals of a company's change-the-business processes are the same as those for the run-the-business side: ensure consistency, allow for better management control and improve efficiency. As opposed to run-the-business, where processes were formalized decades ago, the change-the-business processes for managing project-related activities are more recent. Although there were some forerunners in the 1990s, most organizations did not begin to develop these processes until the early 2000s. Figure 5.4 shows the three most common change-the-business processes.

Project Management

Project management is the central change-the-business process. This methodology comprises a set of standards, templates, roles, responsibilities and governing bodies whose objectives are very similar to those of the run-the-business processes discussed earlier:

- Ensure consistency in the management and the execution of projects.

- Enable comparison of the progress and performance of different projects.

- Improve communication and collaboration between the different entities involved in a project – mainly between the business (e.g., marketing, sales, strategy, finance) and the technical personnel (e.g., IT, engineering, research and development).

- Develop and improve project management competencies within the organization.

- Accelerate the introduction of new products, applications and services.

- Most importantly, to enhance performance and project execution. (Note that a company that successfully executes its projects does not necessarily achieve better results; management also has to choose the right projects in which to invest. This is covered in more detail below.)

A project management methodology is an absolute must for any company that has or plans to have any change-the-business activities. Despite this necessity, and due to the unnoticed and unstoppable trend for increasing project activities, for decades companies had no common methodology and projects were managed ad hoc. The consequences of this lack of standards have been discussed in previous chapters.

Today, there are two main global methodologies: the Project Management Institute's (PMI) *A Guide to the Project Management Body of Knowledge* (better known as the *PMBOK® Guide*)[4] and the UK Office of Government Commerce's (OGC) Prince 2, which stands for Projects in Controlled Environments.[5] These two project management methodologies are not 100 per cent comparable and interchangeable, but they serve the same purpose. My recommendation is that businesses operating in the UK or the Netherlands, especially in the public sector, should consider Prince 2. For businesses based in the US or with extensive international operations, it is better to implement PMI. The largest component of both methodologies is the description of project management processes and templates, which is the basis of project management.

I strongly recommend that the development of a companywide project management methodology begin with the selection of one of the standard methodologies (PMI or Prince 2) as a foundation for benchmarking and

---

4   See http://www.pmi.org.
5   See http://www.prince-officialsite.com.

Table 5.1   Example gap analysis

Process Groups / Knowledge Area	Initiating	Planning	Executing	Controlling	Closing
Project Integration Management					
Project Scope Management					
Project Time Management					
Project Cost Management					
Project Quality Management					
Project Human Resource Management					
Project Communication Management					
Risk Project Management					
Project Procurement Management					

RAG indication: ■ no evidence   ■ some evidence – process defined by one department   ☐ compliance with PMI – company wide process defined

identifying companywide best practices and any weaknesses. Complete a gap analysis (an example is shown in Table 5.1), a tool that helps compare actual and potential performance, whose scope is not only IT department practices but also business department activities. Despite not having a standard methodology, over the years every company has developed best practices in some departments and in some areas of project management.

After completing the gap analysis, keep and consolidate in-house best practices, capture the missing areas from the foundation methodology, and then customize it all to your company needs. Perform a few pilot projects using the new methodology and then fine-tune it using the results. Finally roll it out throughout the change-the-business community using plenty of training and coaching support. This whole exercise can be done in less than two months (if the team is working full time and it is managed like a project).

The benefits of using one of these two project management methodologies is that they evolve and are regularly updated by experts, which then facilitates the improvements to your own methodology. In addition, they offer professional project management certification and open the door to many project management communities.

Programme Management

Like project management, programme management is a set of processes, methods, templates and techniques. Its objectives are to:

- Manage multiple ongoing interdependent projects in the change-the-business dimension.

- Coordinate and prioritize resources across projects, departments and entities to ensure that scarce resources are managed globally.

- Provide a layer above project management that focuses on selecting the best group of initiatives for reaching strategic goals.

- Define projects and provide an infrastructure for successfully running projects while leaving their management to project managers.

A project is a temporary organizational structure that is needed to produce a unique and predefined objective within a specified time and using predetermined resources. A programme, on the other hand, is more permanent and is implemented to consistently achieve certain strategic objectives.

It is important to note that programme management adds another layer of management and some extra bureaucracy to the organization, thus increasing overall costs. However, when a group of projects falls under a programme, the benefits are generally greater than if each project is managed individually.

Unfortunately, projects and programmes often get mixed up because standard methodologies fail to provide clear criteria to distinguish between them. For example, an enterprise resource management (ERP) system implementation is in some cases considered a project and in others a programme. My recommendation is to use the hard criteria shown in Table 5.2 to differentiate between projects and programmes.[6]

Finally, I strongly suggest skipping programme management when beginning the implementation of project management methods. After establishing common project management standards and applying them throughout the organization, employees begin almost naturally to group projects into programmes. In addition, top management starts to break down its strategic objectives into programmes. My experience shows that this phased approach – beginning with project management and then evolving

---

6   This model is not meant to be directive; rather, it is intended to provide some guidance and structure in the change-the-business dimension. Grey areas will develop and will need to be addressed on an ad hoc basis by management and by using common sense.

Table 5.2   **Proposed differentiation between projects and programmes**

	Project	Programme
Cost	< 5m euro	> 5m euro
Impact	Department(s)	Whole company
Duration*	3–18 months	18–240 months
Outcome	Deliverables	Benefits
Frequent Types	New product New methods Initial public offering Departmental system	Merger Integration Transformation Downsizing

Note: This model is not meant to be directive; rather, it is intended to provide some guidance and structure in the change-the-business dimension. Grey zones will develop and will need to be addressed on an ad-hoc basis by management and using common sense; * Projects less than three months in duration should not be considered projects per se. Instead, they should be considered either studies/analyses or activities to keep the run-the-business dimension in good shape.

into programme management – works more effectively than trying to impose both methodologies at the same time. The confusion it creates is difficult to overcome.

Project Portfolio Management

Project portfolio management is the layer that rests on top of all project and programme management activities. It is the cockpit of the change-the-business dimension. Project portfolio management is composed of its own set of processes, templates, techniques, roles and responsibilities, which differ from the project and programme management processes described earlier. The most important aspects of project portfolio management are outlined below.

- A standard and structured *process for collecting all of the new project ideas*. This companywide process must be applied consistently, which makes the next step – comparing project ideas – much easier. Every proposed idea requires a business case and some common qualitative criteria, such as strategic alignment, assessment of risk factors and determination of interdependencies. The ideas for the most strategic projects, such as acquisitions, will often come directly from top management; but management should follow the same process.

- A *procedure for prioritizing and selecting the new project ideas.* Ongoing projects must also be prioritized, particularly the first time the prioritization process is implemented. The selection process has to be fair and transparent, based on criteria against which the new proposal is assessed. Some common criteria for analysing new ideas are net present value (NPV), return on investment (ROI), payback period, strategic alignment, risk and complexity, and interdependencies. One very important selection criterion involves ensuring that the company has the right competencies to deliver the project, which is determined by performing a capability check. I recommend not developing formulas that automate the process of prioritizing and selecting the projects. The exercise is mainly to provide management with different orientations and viewpoints but the ultimate decision has to made by management, based on human intelligence.

- The *strategic roadmap,* which lists the change-the-business dimension's running and new projects for the next two to three years. The company's strategic objectives and goals should be clearly reflected by this roadmap, and the project list should be prioritized so that the top five projects are clearly identified. These top projects usually do not change and are the focus of most of management's attention. The strategic roadmap is communicated and explained throughout the entire organization (see Figure 5.5).

- A *governing body* – the investment decision and execution committee – that decides in which ideas and initiatives the firm will invest and which will be stopped or delayed. The IDEC also approves the company's strategic roadmap for the next two to three years.

- A *gate approval process* that allows for effective portfolio monitoring and control of project funding. This process consists of establishing three to five standard phases for a project's lifecycle – for example, feasibility, initiation, planning, execution and close. At the end of each phase, project feasibility is evaluated and funding is released for the following phase only.

- A *method for monitoring the execution of the strategic roadmap,* which consists mainly of regular reports to top management on the progress of the prioritized projects. If the strategic roadmap is

#	Initiative	Priority		ROI	G	PI	MA	Progress	Gate	Start	End
		S/T	L/T								
P1	CRM – Improve Relationship Management	1	✓		10%	✓	✓		50%	G3	01/06/11	31/03/12
P2	Growth Culture	2		✓	15%	✓	✓		25%	G1	01/10/11	31/06/12
P3	Sectoral Views – Define priority areas	3	✓		7%	✓			75%	G1	01/07/11	31/08/12
P4	Market Intelligence – Improve market watch	4		✓	14%	✓		✓	50%	G5	01/03/11	31/03/12
P5	Private Equity Houses – Build the right alliances	5	✓		-4%	✓			75%	G4	01/10/10	31/03/12
P6	Systems simplification	6	✓		5%			✓	0%	G0	01/01/12	30/06/13
P7	Implementation PPM software	7		✓	6%	✓	✓		75%	G4	01/06/11	30/06/12
P8	New regulatory requirements	8	✓		-10%			✓	0%	G0	01/01/12	31/12/12
P9	Competency – Building the competencies	9		✓	3%	✓			50%	G4	01/06/11	31/03/12

PROJECT TYPES: G: Growth / PI: Productivity Improvement / MA: Mandatory

PROJECT STATUS: R: Resources / C: Cost / Q: Quality / B: Benefits

BENEFITS ACHIEVED

Today

Figure 5.5 Example strategic road map

following the plans, the strategy side of the change-the-business dimension is on track. These regular reports also help management react quickly to market changes and supervise the pipeline of new projects.

- Finally, *a process for capturing the synergies and the benefits of the change-the-business dimension*. As explained in Chapter 3, one of the major issues with projects is that the benefits are difficult to track due primarily to their lack of ownership, the difficulty of measuring them and long time spans (e.g., for some projects, benefits can be achieved only five years after the project has been completed).

    I suggest implementing the benefits-tracking process that I used when managing the integration of companies. During an acquisition, synergies are linked to specific milestones in the integration plans. When a milestone is reached that has synergies attached to it – for example, the closure of some branches – then the benefits can be calculated and compared to the plans. The strategic roadmap has to include these 'synergy-delivering' milestones that are attached to specific returns even if the project has been completed. By doing so, management has a way of monitoring the benefits of the change-the-business dimension.

Focused Organization = Change-the-Business + Run-the-Business

Interconnections between Run-the-Business and Change-the-Business

In order to become a focused organization, the run-the-business and the change-the-business processes and methods must interconnect at certain critical points. If these connection points are missing, the company will remain very strongly unbalanced in the direction of its run-the-business side, as this is generally its dominant dimension. Related to these interconnections are three critical processes that need to be managed transversally across the organization: resource management, budgeting and strategic planning.

Resource Management

Having a clear overview of available resources is critical to determining in which initiatives the company will invest its funds. Ideally, this overview should include competencies: Do company staff have the right skills to carry out the work?

Today, many companies decide to invest in projects without knowing first, whether the resources are available and, second, whether the company has the competencies necessary to successfully complete the project. In addition, most companies that lack resource management processes allow their available capacity, rather than their organizational priorities, to dictate which projects will be launched and when.

Resource management is a very important interconnection between a company's run-the-business and change-the-business dimensions. By providing a clear view of the resources committed and available in both aspects of the company, preferably for a rolling forecast of six quarters, this process enables the investment decision and execution committee to make the best possible decisions about where to invest funds. The run-the-business dimension, despite being the more stable business aspect, also benefits from knowing exactly what resources are available.

One of resource management's major challenges is predicting future needs. Companies are not used to estimating how many resources they will consume for years to come (the budgeting cycle partially estimates this amount per year, but only at full-time equivalent level and mainly for the run-the-business side); and current economic uncertainties, with no one really knowing how the market will look in 6–12 months, render this estimation exercise even more difficult.

The final concern is who should be responsible for the resource management process. Having a single owner of all of the company's resources is too difficult. My recommendation is to have a committee of senior managers that oversees the capacity management process. If skills and competencies are brought into the picture, then the human resources experts should be involved in the process as well. Ultimately, the resource management process should be linked to the competency model.

Businesses should not underestimate the effort involved in getting this process up and running. Implementation can easily take two to three years, and realizing benefits can take much longer.

Budgeting and Accounting

The second interconnection between run-the-business and change-the-business involves budgeting and accounting. The budgeting cycle involves planning the costs, expenses and, where applicable, the revenues for the year to come and then reviewing that plan quarterly. But this process is such a reflection of the past that it is always, or at least until very recently, based solely on the run-the-business dimension. In fact, a separation between run and change activities rarely exists.

Accounting standards and regulations have also focused almost exclusively on the run-the-business segment, providing little guidance on how to deal with project costs and expenses. Neither of the two most important financial statements in today's business – the profit and loss statement and the balance sheet – gives any clear views on the change-the-business dimension. Only very recently has a new accounting standard been introduced that addresses the amortization of project expenses. Its requirements are as follows:

- Once a project reaches certain milestones, direct external and incremental internal project development costs must be amortized on a straight-line basis over the lives of the related project assets (e.g., IT software, construction). Such amortization commences on the date that the asset is put in operation.

- Development costs related to unsuccessful projects are charged to expenses, yet this rule is not black and white and is inconsistent in its application.

This accounting standard is unclear on how the required amortization will affect the total budget allocated for change-the-business activities. Are the unused funds returned to the change-the-business budget, or is the budget reduced? When applied too strictly, project accounting can take the focus away from the pure management of the project.

In order to become a focused organization and be able to monitor how much is spent in each dimension, it is important that these two issues be solved. The accounting standards dealing with project matters should be clarified, simplified and eventually applied by the accounting department, allowing the project manager to focus on leading the project. In addition, the accounting department should explain how to deal with the impact of amortization/depreciation on the overall budgets for both dimensions.

Finally, the accounting department should determine how to address the change-the-business dimension in the budgeting cycle. It can do so by either recategorizing some of the existing costs or by defining new project-specific costs.

Solving these issues is of utmost importance to the accurate reporting of finances, which is very much needed to measure the success of the strategy execution in the achievement of the strategic goals.

Strategic Planning and Strategy Execution

The third interconnected process relates to strategy. In order for a company to successfully execute its strategy, its strategic planning and strategy execution processes must be fully aligned.

Most organizations already have a strategic planning process, but this generally does not distinguish between the run-the-business and change-the-business dimensions. It is critical that these two dimensions be differentiated when the company's strategic objectives are drafted.

On the other hand, strategy execution is a process that very few companies have defined or implemented. This is not an issue of bad management only; rather, as opposed to other management practices, this lacks globally recognized definitions and standards. While researching business schools and MBA programmes, I did not find any courses dealing exclusively with strategy execution. Nor did I find much related literature, which is the opposite of what would be the case if I researched strategic planning. I struggle to understand why such a core process as strategy execution, which is fundamental to every organization, has been so neglected.

As shown in Figure 5.6, the strategy execution process must address the objectives and monitor the progress of both the run-the-business and the change-the-business dimensions. Run-the-business objectives are mainly short term and comprise commercial and operational targets, whereas change-the-business strategic goals are mostly longer term. Successfully achieving run-the-business targets is the company's priority and is vital to any investment in change-the-business goals. The strategy execution process thus comprises a combination of all these steps.

Systems and Tools

None of the above improvements can be achieved without a set of critical systems and tools that support the execution and management of both the run-the-business and the change-the-business components.

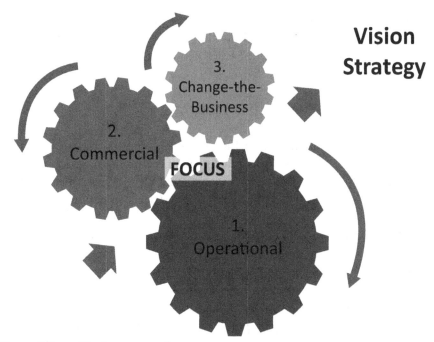

Figure 5.6   Strategy execution

RUN-THE-BUSINESS

The key systems and tools that support the run-the-business dimension are usually well established. Some of these applications are more mature than others, but the biggest improvements in automation have already been achieved. I consider the enterprise resource planning (ERP) systems implementations begun in the late 1980s to be the start of the modern automation of the run-the-business dimension and the neglect of the change-the-business component.

Reaching the present level of systems and tools maturity has taken companies more than three decades and has generally been very painful and costly. Many projects failed or took much longer than foreseen; costs tripled or quadrupled beyond the original estimations; and the promised benefits were either never achieved or were achieved much later than the vendor and consulting companies promised in order to win the pitch. My opinion is that these large, troublesome projects left management with deep scars which were then reflected for years to come in a lack of appreciation for project management and its value to IT and technical projects.

The value chain elements listed in Chapter 1 help to map the company's run-the-business systems and to show that both core and support processes have solid systems behind them. Some of the core applications in the run dimension are discussed below.

Enterprise Resource Planning (ERP) Systems

The fundamental advantage of an ERP system is that it integrates business data from many of the business's management, core and support processes into a single application. This helps management have better control of their business, increases productivity and allows better decision making.

ERP applications usually cover the backbone of the organization, including supply chain, logistics, manufacturing, material management, inventory management, distribution and accounting. Management uses the most relevant business information to run the organization on a daily basis. Not every company has an ERP system: some have their own in-house developed applications; others have implemented just a few modules from one of the standard packages and implemented other types of applications around them. Although they are relatively new, ERP systems don't address the change-the-business dimension and all project-related activities.

Commercial Systems

Commercial systems cover the business's commercial and client relationship management activities. They are essential to managing sales and all customer-related (existing and potential) information. Some ERP packages provide this commercial functionality too.

The past decade has seen an explosion of e-commerce systems which involve using a website to promote and sell a company's services and products. But one thing is clear: these systems do not cover change-the-business activities.

Financial Reporting Systems

All of the company's accounting and financial information must be consolidated into a financial system, which is then used to produce the official statutory reports that regulators and shareholders require. In conjunction with this system, companies need a solid budgeting and forecasting process that is supported by specific software. Either the financial or the budgetary system covers the change-the-business dimension.

People Management Systems

Human resources is an important area in every company. The automation in HR has concentrated primarily on back office activities, such as payroll and staff information, which can also be automated through the ERP system. The more strategic parts of HR – such as rewards, learning and development – have also been automated, but their maturity level is lower and can be improved.

Business Management Reporting Systems

In addition to the core and the supporting processes, management-related processes have been automated. So-called 'management information' or 'business intelligence' applications provide consolidated information to middle and top management to control and manage their departments and resources on a day-to-day basis. The strategic planning process is often also supported by an application.

CHANGE-THE-BUSINESS

The change and project side of the business is much less mature than the run dimension, and hardly any of the tools related to managing this increasingly more critical dimension have been in place for long. If we look at the tools available to support the three key change-the-business systems – project management, programme management and project portfolio management – we will see that each of them has a different situation.

Project Management System

Thanks to Microsoft and its MS Project software,[7] project management has extended throughout many organizations. Like the other three Microsoft Office applications – Excel, Word and PowerPoint – MS Project is a highly intuitive and flexible tool that can be used after less than an hour's practice, albeit at only a fraction of its functionality. MS Project has had a positive impact in that with one simple-to-use tool project managers can more or less easily manage their projects. The downside is that it is an end-user tool, thus not centralized, and every project manager has his or her own way of using it and planning projects. Consequently, individual project plans are not comparable and are difficult to consolidate for the purpose of reporting to management.

---

7   See http://www.microsoft.com/project.

Besides MS Project, there are many other project management applications,[8] such as GanttProject[9] or BaseCamp.[10] The key challenge is selecting the right project management tool, which I feel should incorporate project portfolio management functionality.

Programme Management System

There is actually no tool, per se, to fully support programme management. Because programme management exists in theory somewhere between project management and portfolio management, but in practice is closer to the latter, the project management software discussed above is what is most commonly used. As the difference between project and programme is not too clear, I therefore recommend focusing on project management and using the related tool.

Project Portfolio Management System

Using a companywide project portfolio management system is indispensable to managing the change-the-business dimension. Managing hundreds of projects, thousands of resources and millions of euro without such tools as Excel, MS Project and PowerPoint is unimaginable; but this is what most companies are still doing. Until recently, companies had no control of their change-the-business dimension and had little idea of either the total costs invested or the expected benefits. I call this a 'black box' situation.

Over the past five years this situation has changed, accelerated by the financial crisis of 2009. Many companies have now turned to PPM processes and tools to:

- Gain control of all projects and project-related activities.

- Move from the 'black box' to a transparent environment, creating visibility and producing accurate data.

- Reduce costs by cutting spending on projects and reducing project-related overhead through such measures as eliminating PMOs and investing in fewer initiatives.

---

8   A good overview can be found at http://en.wikipedia.org/wiki/Comparison_of_project_mana gement_software.
9   See http://www.ganttproject.biz.
10   See http://basecamphq.com.

- Accelerate change in the organization to adapt to the current volatility of the environment and to survive the economic crisis.

- Improve project execution and increase the overall efficiency of the change-the-business dimension.

The PPM tools provide functionality in the following areas: innovation management, investment management, prioritization of ideas, selection of projects, scenario simulation, project management and follow-up, capacity/ resource management and project financial management. Particularly in the last two areas the PPM tools have tried to link the run and the change dimensions but, unfortunately, linking these two sides is not possible.

Trying to capture all the change-the-business elements in one tool creates the risk that instead of being fully dedicated to managing projects and the overall portfolio of projects, the tool is used mainly for time tracking and resource management or, even worse, for project accounting because the financial aspects become most important.

With the increased demand for PPM tools, most of the big IT software vendors have moved into this area by acquiring the original PPM tools. Two technology research and consulting companies, Gartner[11] and Forrester,[12] assess the different tools in the market. Gartner's magic quadrant is famous throughout IT departments, which have been primarily responsible for driving the implementation of PPM tools. The main reason for this is that IT generally runs more projects and has more mature project management practices than other departments within an organization.

Despite this increase in PPM implementations, many of them have taken much longer than anticipated; have been more costly than initially planned; and have not fully delivered the vendor-promised benefits. This is very similar to what happened two decades ago with the implementation of ERPs. The main reasons why PPM tools are so difficult to implement are: outlined below.

- The IT department, which drives the implementation, creates a lack of buy-in and the tool is used by less than half of the organization.

---

11 See http://www.gartner.com/technology/research.jsp.
12 See http://www.forrester.com/rb/research.

The business itself, preferably via a cross-departmental team, has to sponsor and lead the roll-out of a PPM tool.

- The very expensive PPM application is turned into a time-tracking tool.

Today, most PPM implementations begin by asking all employees working in the change-the-business dimension to register their hours on timesheets. This approach, which is the worst I can imagine, creates enemies and resistance to using the PPM application and causes many organizations to use it to track staff hours. A PPM tool should be implemented using a top-down approach, focusing first on the organization's strategy and priorities and on the projects that are currently running. By creating clarity on the top, the value of the tool is visible more quickly, increasing the buy-in for the implementation.

- Mature processes are lacking and the segments of the organization are misaligned.

Often, companies decide to implement a PPM tool without having first defined and rolled out the project, programme and portfolio management processes. In addition, organizational changes and alignment have not yet taken place, so the PPM tool is implemented without having a strong foundation and therefore does not stay in place for long.

If the company begins by defining and implementing the change-the-business processes and performing the organizational changes needed to support those new processes, implementing the PPM application will be much easier. Users will welcome the tool, as it will make their work easier.

- The PPM tool is not connected with the run-the-business dimension.

PPM tools do not connect easily with the run dimension's key processes and data. Although they claim to be all-in-one tools that can be used for both defining and executing strategy, this is not the case. As a result, company management does not recognize their added value or support their implementation. The

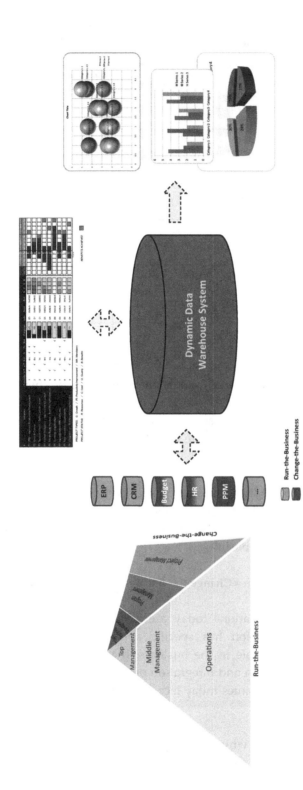

Figure 5.7   Strategy execution application

Table 5.3   Example of data included in a strategy execution system

Application	Data	Dimension
ERP	Sales forecast and actuals Cost planning and actuals ...	Run-the-Business
CRM	Customer profitability Market analysis ...	Run-the-Business
Budgeting	Budgets Forecast ...	Both
HR	Manpower allocation Capabilities ...	Both
PPM	Strategic priorities Project estimates and actuals Earned values/benefits ...	Change-the-Business
Other	...	...

marketing of PPM tools should therefore focus on their ability to automate project and portfolio management and should not try to oversell their functionality. If the automation of the change-the-business dimension is done well, this is already a very big step in performance.

Notwithstanding all these issues, sooner or later every organization will need to implement a PPM tool to manage all its change-the-business and project activities. There is no other way to get the transparency needed to manage this large and critical part of the business.

Focused Organization = Change-the-Business + Run-the-Business

As we have seen, organizations today are composed of an amalgam of applications. Each dimension has specific applications that are needed to efficiently perform its role in the business. If we consider that strategy execution is the combination and integration of the run and the change, then we can conclude that companies today lack the software to plan and execute their strategies.

This is one of the reasons why strategy execution is so difficult and although many vendors claim to have produced a strategy execution tool, this is not the

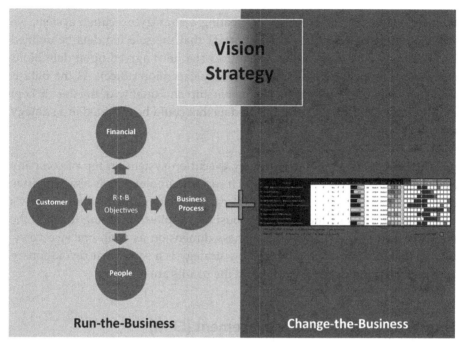

Figure 5.8   Enterprise performance management

case. In fact, there is no single tool that can cover both sides of the business and consolidate the information to allow management to follow up the execution of their strategies. For me, the strategy execution tool has not yet been invented. On the other hand, being regularly confronted with the lack of such a tool has led me to find a temporary solution that I believe should form the basis for its future development.

This temporary solution involves building a *strategy execution system* based on a dynamic enriched data warehouse with simulation functionalities (Figure 5.7). The data warehouse connects to all the relevant systems used in the run- and the change-the-business dimension and extracts only the relevant data needed for management to build and follow up on the strategy. The tool also establishes controls on the quality of the data, monitoring the accuracy of the information but ensuring that the data is corrected at the source.

The sources of this data are critical since only a selection of relevant information is extracted to be worked on and enriched in the data warehouse. A large multinational can easily have thousands of pieces of business, operational and project data, with definitions that can differ depending on the owner and the user. However, for purposes of creating a strategy execution system, we will look at just a selection. It is important that the selected data be defined in a companywide data model which uses standard agreed-upon definitions and is kept in a centralized entity (strategy execution office). As the data is extracted from the applications, the ownership and quality of the data is kept locally. Table 5.3 shows an example of data that could be included in a strategy execution system.

The benefits of building a strategy execution system on top of company applications are that the system is much easier to implement; is less expensive than any other software package; and can be customized to the company's specific needs. It is neither a run-the-business application trying to cover the particularities of the change-the-business dimension as well, nor vice versa. I know that this approach to building a strategy is a somewhat revolutionary approach but I have seen it work – and the results are amazing.

Enterprise Performance Management (EPM)

Enterprise performance management refers to a framework (e.g., processes, tools, key performance indicators) that manages performance and measures it against the company's predefined operational, commercial and strategic goals. Some well-known performance management methodologies include Total Quality Management (TQM), Economic Value Added (EVA), Six Sigma (6Σ) and Activity Based Costing (ABC); but the one that is most widely used is the Balanced Scorecard, which was developed in 1992 by Robert Kaplan and David Norton. The main drawback of the Balanced Scorecard and the other enterprise performance management methodologies is that they address only the run-the-business dimension, thus failing to account for a large and key element of strategy execution.

Enterprise performance management is a top-down framework that focuses on managing the execution of the firm's strategic goals. As shown in Figure 5.8, it covers both run-the-business and change-the-business dimensions and monitors the execution of the commercial and operational goals, together with the company's strategic roadmap.

EPM uses the Balanced Scorecard approach because it is the best methodology for measuring the performance of the run-the-business dimension. For the change-the-business dimension, I use the strategic roadmap. The combination of the balanced scorecard and the strategic roadmap completes the picture and makes the follow-up of the strategy execution possible.

CONCLUSION

It is important to highlight that in order to achieve the full benefit of becoming a focused organization, all six elements described in this chapter should be seamlessly linked. In the next and last chapter of this book, I will discuss how to achieve this integration.

6

How to Implement a Focused Organization

Fundamental transformations, such as changing the company's values and culture, always require big investment of time, money and effort; and their benefits are very difficult to quantify. Often, the benefits are of the so-called 'soft' – or intangible – variety, such as an improvement in motivation or the creation of an entrepreneurial mindset. The hard benefits, like cost savings or revenue increases, are frequently not concrete. In addition, gains are generally achieved in the medium to long term, usually after three to five years of hard work.

Because chief executive officers (CEOs) and top management receive substantial pressure from shareholders and the stock markets to quickly and regularly show positive returns on their investments, they are reluctant to embark on these types of initiatives. Instead, they prefer to invest in acquisitions or downsizing projects, which pay off much more quickly and have a tangible impact on the bottom line.

Usually, the parallel launch of a transformation project and a strategic project is what top management regards as the most attractive scenario. This is a controllable situation if management focuses just on these two initiatives. However, as explained before, they end up launching too many strategic projects simultaneously or in a short time period, which is a recipe for failure.

This final chapter describes in practical terms the steps necessary to become a focused organization. To overcome this transformation project's two major drawbacks – intangible benefits and a delay in achieving them – I have developed a fast-track approach that provides top management with quantifiable results in less than 12 months. To achieve the full benefits of a focused organization the transformation has to be consolidated and the changes have to be fully embedded in the company.

Now let us look at the main steps that need to be taken to become a focused organization.

Ensure That the CEO and Top Management Fully Support the Initiative

The first step in becoming a focused organization is for the CEO and top management to fully understand the rationale for the change and to accept that the company exhibits some or most of the following symptoms of being unfocused.

- A lack of:

    - information on how well the company is implementing its strategy;

    - clarity about how the strategic goals will be achieved (absence of focus and discipline throughout the entire organization);

    - company priorities;

    - visibility about the number of projects, their status, actual cost, estimated completion cost, benefits and business case;

    - data on the status of the projects – status reports take weeks to produce and never show accurate information.

- Projects are initiated by individual departments without proper analysis and a clear business case.

- Impossibility of comparing different projects.

- Increased numbers of companywide projects, with many more projects being started than are completed.

- Unclear ownership of the different projects and portfolio of projects.

- Absence of a cross-departmental governing body that decides in which projects to invest and ensures that projects are correctly executed.

- Poor communication and collaboration between the business and the IT department when defining the project.

- An impression that the programme management offices are bureaucratic, with low added value to the company.

- Non-existence of an integrated tool to manage the change-the-business dimension; if such a tool does exist, it is not correctly used or most of its functionality is unavailable.

- Increasingly long lead times to develop and launch new products to market.

In addition to acknowledging some or all of the above issues, management needs to be willing to make the effort to change fundamental aspects of the organization. If this awareness is missing and an urgency to change is not felt, then it is best not to start the project.

Make the Project a Priority and Allocate the Best Resources

Top management's recognition of the need for change is not enough to successfully carry out the process of becoming focused. What is also necessary is top management's leadership of, and active involvement in, this transformation project.

In fact, the focused organization transformation project (FOTP) steering committee should be composed of executive committee members. The sponsor of the project must be either the company's CEO (preferably) or the equivalent, such as the chief operations officer (COO) or the chief finance officer (CFO).

As stated earlier, the CIO should not be the project sponsor in order to avoid lack of buy-in from the business and commercial departments. However, the CIO should be part of the steering committee and must be able to dedicate several hours a week to the transformation project. The same commitment is required from the members of the steering committee. Besides being an active part of the FOTP, top management needs to lead by example and apply early on some of the new key principles to their day-to-day work.

In addition, the FOTP has to be close to the top of the list of company endeavours. It should not be the first and most important because that position should always be filled by a revenue growth or profitability-related strategic project. Because the business likely does not rank its projects, a good indication of project importance is the amount of time that top management dedicates to the project and the level within the organization of the sponsor and the members of the steering committee.

Once the sense of urgency has been established, the project sponsor has been appointed and the project has been prioritized, a project manager needs to be selected. This choice should not be too time-consuming, but the project manager should be one of the best and most skilful members of the organization rather than someone who is simply readily available. Eventually, the project manager could also be an external consultant, someone who understands the complexity of becoming a focused organization and who has already completed such a transformation. Selecting someone from outside the organization often works better because he or she can directly confront any pockets of resistance without being biased or influenced by internal agendas. As resistance levels are sometimes high and critical issues have to be addressed quickly, it is important that the project manager be persuasive and unafraid of expressing views that differ from those of top management. Finally, it is imperative that the project manager be 120 per cent dedicated to the project.

As soon as the project manager has been appointed, the rest of the project team has to be selected. The core team should be composed of five to eight people who are also dedicated full time to the project, as well as experts from each affected department who will share best practices, participate in the defining methodologies, validate processes and tools and then lead the adoption of the new model in their business units. Department representatives need to dedicate at least 50, rather than 100, per cent of their time to the project.

After the team has been appointed, the next step for the project manager is to draw up a high-level project plan that identifies key milestones and primary workstreams. It is important to highlight that the project should last no more than one year, and preferably a few months less than that.

As indicated in Figure 6.1, the high-level plan needs to be concise, action oriented, fast and focused. A significant part of the plan is dedicated to

Focused Organization Transformation project

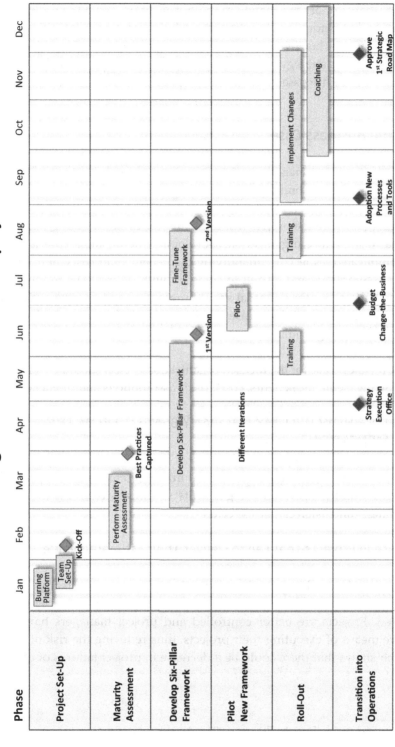

Figure 6.1   High-level project plan

activities that support the change in the organization. Once the project nears completion, but before the changes are put into operation, a transitional plan should be set up. This involves turning over coordination of the project to the newly established strategy execution office (SEO). The role of the SEO during this phase will be discussed later in this chapter.

Build the Business Case

One of the project manager's first tasks is to work with the project sponsor and other experts to build the business case for the focused organization transformation project (FOTP). Having a clear business case is essential for estimating the value the project will bring and for communicating and selling the idea to the entire organization. Developing the business case is always very complicated, especially quantifying the benefits and costs, and involves making assumptions and daring to come up with figures. The numbers will never be perfect, but the proposal should present a good approximation. The qualitative side of the business case is easier and is, in fact, very similar to that of most of the change initiatives.

The business case for the focused organization project should cover at least the following elements: benefits, costs, risks, assumptions and financials.

BENEFITS – HOW WILL MY COMPANY BENEFIT FROM THE IMPLEMENTATION?

Each level of the organization will benefit in a different way, as explained in Figure 6.2. In addition, the following benefits[1] specifically related to the change-the-business dimension can be expected:

Decrease in Projects That Fail to Deliver Their Estimated Value

By becoming focused, companies ensure that projects are correctly selected, properly resourced, precisely executed and monitored until the benefits are delivered. Projects are better controlled and project managers have more effective means of executing their projects, thus reducing the risk of failure. Research shows that there could be a decrease in project failures of about 15 per cent.

---

1   Figures are based on Forrester Research 2009 and personal experience.

Figure 6.2   Business case – qualitative benefits

Reduction in Project Cost Overruns

By investing in fewer projects and increasing the transparency of project information, management will be able to better control project-related spending. In addition, by establishing standard procedures and enforcing the preparation of a business case before a new initiative is approved, estimation of costs and benefits will improve significantly. Best practices show that the rate of cost overruns can be reduced by 10 per cent.

Faster Time to Market

The increase in visibility, the use of common standards and the implementation of a common tool will provide top management with faster and more accurate information for decision making. Quicker decision making together with fewer projects that are better staffed will reduce project duration, which means shorter time to market for revenue-generating projects and thus faster access to potential revenues. Studies show that project duration can decrease by approximately 10 per cent.

Fewer Low-value and Redundant Projects

By developing a process for capturing all new improvement and growth ideas and potential projects, top management has much better control of which projects to invest in (or not). This allows management to compare new ideas across the different departments and to choose those projects that bring the highest returns to the entire business. Those low-value projects that in the past would be started without being challenged will now be disregarded. Finally, from the hundreds of projects that a large company has running at any point, at least 10–20 per cent can be cancelled easily without serious impact on the business.

Decrease in Resources Dedicated to Change-the-Business

Both internal and external resources dedicated to project-related activities can be reduced. The organizational alignment that takes place improves significantly the way the change-the-business dimension is organized and the transparency created allows better management of project-related resources. Programme management offices become less populated and much more efficient. External resources, which by definition are involved in change-the-business projects and often are twice as expensive as the internal ones, are significantly reduced. In addition, resources are trimmed down because of the speed at which the organization is becoming more focused. The savings in resources can run at 10–15 per cent.

COSTS – HOW MUCH WILL THE FOCUSED ORGANIZATION TRANSFORMATION PROJECT COST, INCLUDING IMPLEMENTATION AND ROLLOUT? HOW MUCH WILL IT COST TO RUN THE NEW ORGANIZATIONAL MODEL?

The implementation of the new organization will generate two different types of costs.

Transformation Project Costs

These charges are related to the people, resources and length of time involved in running the project. Usually, five to eight people, excluding the project manager, comprise the core project team. In addition, each department dedicates two to three resources to the project. The project lasts six–12 months, depending on the size of the company. Other main project costs are associated with:

- the project portfolio management tool – including customization and implementation.

- the strategy execution tool – including development and implementation.

- the coaching and training needed for the rollout – estimated at three days training and two days coaching per project manager. Additional training will be needed for top and middle management as well as other people involved in change-the-business, such as resource managers or finance staff.

Costs to Run the New Organization

The costs to run the new organization are associated with:

- The strategy execution office, which usually consists of six to eight people.

- The resources dedicated in each department to follow and to support the new processes and tools.

- The network of programme management offices established around the organization.

- The annual licence fees and maintenance of the project portfolio management tool.

- The annual licence fees and maintenance of the strategy execution tool.

- Ongoing coaching – consider two extra coaching days per project manager per year.

RISKS – WHAT ARE THE MAJOR RISKS IN THE JOURNEY TO BECOME A FOCUSED ORGANIZATION?

As with any large business transformation, carrying out the FOTP entails significant probable risks that project managers need to actively monitor. The most important of these risks are as follows.

Weakened Top Management Support

Top management's attention and support is not unlimited. If the transformation encounters major resistance the benefits take longer to be achieved; or if another more important strategic initiative appears in the landscape, such as a merger, there is the risk that top management support will fade away. This could seriously endanger the success of the transformation project.

Opposition to Implementing the New Organizational and Governing Structure

The organizational changes brought by the FOTP are brutal. Significant power, some resources and portions of the budgets will shift from the run-the-business to the change-the-business dimension. In addition, the focused organization blocks individualism while strongly enforcing the 'one company' spirit.

Lack of Discipline to Enforce Use of the New Methods and Tools

As part of the FOTP implementation, several project management-related processes, templates and tools will be deployed that will change the way people work. These new standards will temporarily increase the workload and right from the start employees will resist following them. Management must be disciplined and have zero tolerance for this resistance. It is important that the entire organization apply these new processes; if not, the decision-making process will be hampered.

Resistance to Increasing Transparency and Sharing Information

Transparency is very uncomfortable for some managers because it brings important information to the surface – such the status of some projects or bad decision making – and allows top management to assess and compare individual managers' capabilities. This results in a huge 'invisible' resistance to becoming transparent, which top management needs to counter by being firm and advocating transparency's benefits.

Failure to Agree the First Roadmap

The first investment decision and execution committee (IDEC) will take place shortly after the project turns into operations, the aim being that at the end of the committee there is a validated roadmap which includes the list of prioritized projects, the approval of some of the ideas (not all) and maybe the cancellation of some running projects. As it will be the first time that top management sits together to discuss the importance of the current portfolio, there is a very high risk that intensive discussions will take place. If at the end of the first IDEC no decision is reached, the image of lack of team spirit projected to the rest of the organization will be extremely negative and will place the entire transformation at stake.

ASSUMPTIONS – WHAT IS THE CURRENT SITUATION AND WHICH VARIABLES SHOULD BE CONSIDERED?

To build the business case, the information outlined in Table 6.1 needs to be available. For most of the organizations I have worked with, this data was

Table 6.1   Business case – assumptions

Estimate	Description	Example Model
Number of running projects	Projects currently active in the company. Usually difficult to identify.	450 projects
Average project costs	Budget dedicated to projects. As companies don't have this information, they will need to make assumptions.	€900,000
Average cycle time	Average duration of the projects, from idea until launch.	14 months
Cost of capital	For an investment to be worthwhile, the return on investment needs to be higher than the cost of capital.	10%
Expected return on investment	Expected return on investment should be some percentage higher than the company's cost of capital.	15%
Number of staff working on change-the-business activities	Total number of internal full-time employees who currently work on project-related activities.	3.000 FTE
Number of external resources associated with change-the-business activities	Total number of external consultants currently working on project-related activities.	1.000 FTE
Average fee paid per day for external resources	The average daily fee that the organization is charged by the external consultants.	€1,000
Estimated cost of the focused organization transformation project	Total cost of the transformation project, including internal staff, external resources, training, and coaching activities.	€1,500,000
Estimated cost of running the change-the-business organization	Total recurring cost of running the change the business dimension, including the dedicated resources and external staff (excluding the total investment in projects).	€380,000,000
Estimated cost of implementing the different tools	Total costs of developing and customizing the project portfolio management tool and the strategy execution tool.	€1,000,000
Estimated costs of licenses and of maintaining the different tools	Yearly license and maintenance costs linked to the use of the project portfolio management tool.	€500,000

either not readily available or not available at all. Thus, I recommend making assumptions and trying to get the best estimates.[2]

FINANCIALS – WHAT ARE THE CONCRETE BENEFITS EXPECTED FROM THE INVESTMENT IN THE FOCUSED ORGANIZATION TRANSFORMATION PROJECT?

The benefits expected from the transformation into a focused organization are both qualitative and quantitative. The qualitative benefits have already been mentioned and the quantitative benefits are explained in Table 6.2.

Table 6.2   Business case – financial benefits

Key Assumptions	Today
Number of running projects:	450
Average investment per project:	€900,000
Average project cycle (months):	14
Total investment in projects:	€405,000,000
Expected Return on Investment	17%
Expected Value Creation from all projects	€68,850,000
Cost of Capital:	10%

Improvements by becoming Focused	Target	Today
Projects not delivering benefits :	10%	15%
Projects running above budget :	20%	35%
Average budget overrun :	10%	
Reduction project cycle time:	20%	
Low-value/redundant projects :	5%	10%

Change-the-Business Resources	Today
Percentage internals vs. externals:	25%
Number of internals:	2,000
Price internals per day:	€500
Average mdays per year per internal:	180
Estimated cost for internals:	€180,000,000
Estimated reduction Internals:	2%
Number of externals:	1,000
Price externals per day:	€1,000
Average mdays per year per external:	200
Estimated cost for externals:	€200,000,000
Estimated reduction externals:	5%
Total Yearly Costs – Change-the-Business	€380,000,000

---

2   A key characteristic of building a business case is that you do not spend months trying to find the data; so do some research, talk to experts and dare to plug in the figures.

Table 6.2   Continued

BENEFITS	2012	2013	2014	Total	NPV
Decrease projects not delivering benefits:	€0	€2,025,000	€10,125,000	€12,150,000	€9,280,616
Savings from less budget overruns:	€0	€121,500	€607,500	€729,000	€556,837
Shorter project cycle:	€0	€578,571	€2,892,857	€3,471,429	€2,651,605
Savings in low-value/redundant projects:	€0	€2,025,000	€10,125,000	€12,150,000	€9,280,616
Reduction in CtB resources:	€0	€4,600,000	€8,600,000	€13,600,000	€10,262,960
TOTAL	€0	€9,350,071	€32,350,357	€42,100,429	€32,032,634

COSTS – PROJECT	2012	2013	2014	Total	NPV
External resources:	€1,000,000	€0	€0	€1,000,000	€909,091
Internal resources:	€500,000	€0	€0	€500,000	€454,545
Strategy Execution Tool Development:	€1,000,000	€0	€0	€1,000,000	€909,091
Strategy Execution Licenses:	€500,000	€0	€0	€500,000	€454,545
TOTAL	€3,000,000	€0	€0	€3,000,000	€2,727,273

COSTS – RUNNING	2012	2013	2014	Total	NPV
Strategy Execution Office Team	€300,000	€800,000	€800,000	€1,900,000	€1,534,936
Extra Support:	€0	€100,000	€100,000	€200,000	€157,776
TOTAL RUNNING	€300,000	€900,000	€900,000	€2,100,000	€1,692,712

| TOTAL | €3,300,000 | €900,000 | €900,000 | €5,100,000 | €4,419,985 |

	2012	2013	2014	Total	NPV
Net Cash Flow	-€3,300,000	€8,450,071	€31,450,357	€37,000,429	€27,612,649
Cumulative Cash Flow:	-€3,300,000	€5,150,071	€36,600,429		
Percent Return on Investment:				725%	

Considering only the financial aspects in this example, investing approximately €3.3 million in such project performance improvements as running fewer processes more efficiently would generate benefits of more than €37 million. But besides the financial benefits of becoming a focused organization, the biggest benefits by far are to be able to execute the strategy and have people fully engaged in the company.

Finally, the business case should be validated by the project sponsor and approved by the steering committee.

Perform a Maturity Assessment

After the business case has been completed and validated by the steering committee, the next step is to perform a maturity assessment instead of the more traditional 'as-is' analysis. A maturity assessment:

- Aims to identify and capture the best practices already in use in the company.

- Allows the construction of a customized approach specific to the needs of the company.

- Facilitates the establishment of incremental improvement targets.

The approach I suggest using to perform the maturity assessment is based on the focused organization framework, which is composed of the six pillars explained in Chapter 4. The second area covers the different levels of the change-the-business dimension and includes the main characteristics of the focused organization as described in Figure 6.3.

The maturity assessment usually takes three to four weeks to complete. I suggest starting with project management and then moving up to project portfolio management. Collect all the project management-related information in the six different areas. Identify those departments that have documented standard practices of managing their projects. Assess whether any department uses a specific tool for managing projects and whether the tool has been developed in-house or is third-party software. Look at the way each department is organized to manage its projects and if it has established a programme management office. Identify whether there is specific training for project management, consisting of different levels and not just one-off. Assess the cultural aspects and the leadership style of each department. Finally, look at the reports used to monitor the different project aspects, such as actual spending and actual progress.

An accelerated way of collecting and validating first impressions is to conduct workshops with experts from the different areas of the affected departments. The same approach should be followed for project portfolio management and for any focused organization elements that the company may already have in place. Figure 6.4 shows an example of outcome of the maturity assessment.

The company has some areas that are well developed across all departments and simply need to be linked to other areas and dimensions. In addition, there are best practices that need to be expanded companywide, with the goal of leveraging those practices rather than throwing them out – which is what some methodologies and consultants would advise. The focus of the project needs to be on those areas where nothing is available.

Fully Develop the Six Pillars of the Focused Organization

A big advantage of completing the maturity assessment is that it allows for customized and accelerated development of the six pillars. The customized approach facilitates buy-in, while the accelerated development generates focus and hard benefits much more quickly.

It is very important to understand that the development process I propose is 'brutal': instead of taking three to five years, with the full benefits being achieved years later, it transforms the organization in less than a year. This acceleration will create tension and will increase the risk of burn-out; however, my experience shows that this process is the best way to create a focused organization. As stated earlier, the work that it takes to become focused must be painful, otherwise the change will be just superficial and will fade away.

If the project team is experienced and has sufficient resources, the six pillars can be fully developed in four to six months. This means that:

- Those areas having a procedure or practice that is used by all departments in the company (lighter grey boxes in the maturity assessment, Figure 6.4) do not need to change. For example, a project management methodology that is applied to all the organization's projects does not need to be addressed in our accelerated development plan. The only step that needs to be taken is to ensure that these companywide procedures and practices are connected to the other pillars, to the other level (in this example, project portfolio management) and to the run-the-business dimension.

- Standard procedures or common practices that are used in only one department (medium grey boxes in the maturity assessment, Figure 6.4) need to be expanded and adapted to the company's other departments. For example, if the IT department has a well-established tool to manage resources and perform capacity

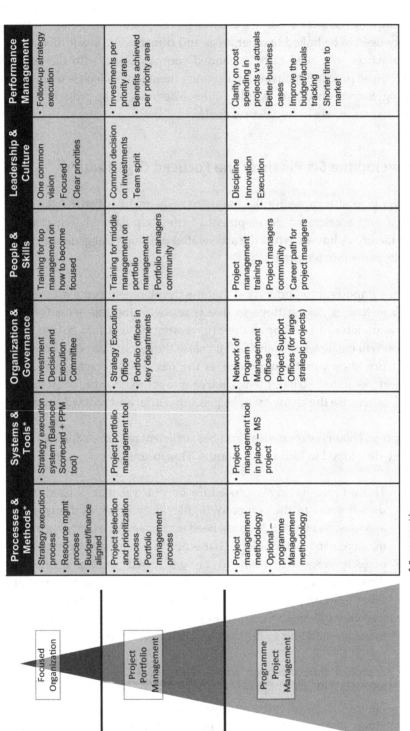

Processes & Methods*	Systems & Tools*	Organization & Governance	People & Skills	Leadership & Culture	Performance Management
• Strategy execution process • Resource mgmt process • Budget/finance aligned	• Strategy execution system (Balanced Scorecard + PPM tool)	• Investment Decision and Execution Committee	• Training for top management on how to become focused	• One common vision • Focused • Clear priorities	• Follow-up strategy execution
• Project selection and prioritization process • Portfolio management process	• Project portfolio management tool	• Strategy Execution Office • Portfolio offices in key departments	• Training for middle management on portfolio management • Portfolio managers community	• Common decision on investments • Team spirit	• Investments per priority area • Benefits achieved per priority area
• Project management methodology • Optional – programme Management methodology	• Project management tool in place – MS project	• Network of Program Management Offices • Project Support Offices (for large strategic projects)	• Project management training • Project managers community • Career path for project managers	• Discipline • Innovation • Execution	• Clarity on cost spending in projects vs actuals • Better business cases • Improve the budget/actuals tracking • Shorter time to market

Focused Organization

Project Portfolio Management

Programme Project Management

* Company wide

Figure 6.3   Maturity model

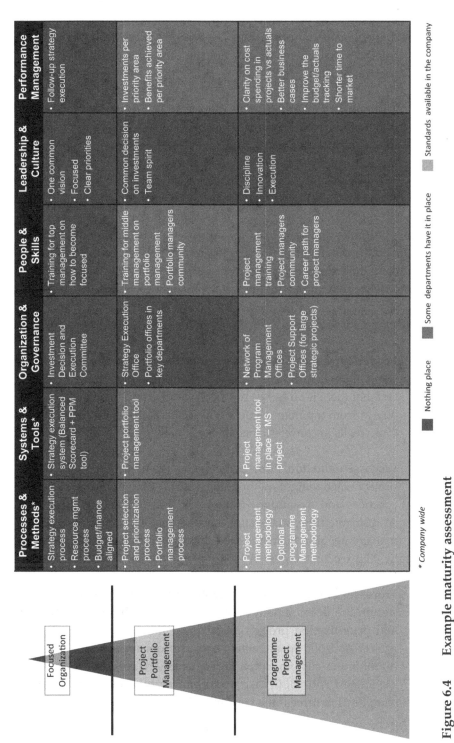

	Processes & Methods*	Systems & Tools*	Organization & Governance	People & Skills	Leadership & Culture	Performance Management
Focused Organization	• Strategy execution process • Resource mgmt process • Budget/finance aligned	• Strategy execution system (Balanced Scorecard + PPM tool)	• Investment Decision and Execution Committee	• Training for top management on how to become focused	• One common vision • Focused • Clear priorities	• Follow-up strategy execution
Project Portfolio Management	• Project selection and prioritization process • Portfolio management process	• Project portfolio management tool	• Strategy Execution Office • Portfolio offices in key departments	• Training for middle management on portfolio management • Portfolio managers community	• Common decision on investments • Team spirit	• Investments per priority area • Benefits achieved per priority area
Programme Project Management	• Project management methodology • Optional – programme Management methodology	• Project management tool in place – MS project	• Network of Program Management Offices • Project Support Offices (for large strategic projects)	• Project management training • Project managers community • Career path for project managers	• Discipline • Innovation • Execution	• Clarity on cost spending in projects vs actuals • Better business cases • Improve the budget/actuals tracking • Shorter time to market

* Company wide

Nothing place   Some departments have it in place   Standards available in the company

Figure 6.4   Example maturity assessment

planning, then this tool should become the standard and should be implemented companywide. The tool may need to be customized to other departments' needs, but the core functionality should not change.

- Those pillars that are not developed at all (the darkest grey boxes in the maturity assessment, Figure 6.4), which will be the majority, need to be based on best practices outside the company. For instance, if the company wants to develop a project portfolio management process, the best way to go about it is to look at the already established PMI (*PMBOK® Guide*) and Prince 2 methodologies.

To maximize efficiency and speed, I propose having a structured and prioritized implementation approach rather than trying to address all six pillars at once. Figure 6.5 shows the sequence of steps in this structured approach and describes the unique benefits associated with the development of each area.

The development sequence, as indicated in the chart, should be as follows:

1. **Leadership and culture**. First, cultivate a common vision which starts at the top and cascades down through the organization. The fact that there is already a burning platform and the project has full buy-in from top management will facilitate this step. Allow two to four weeks to complete this phase.

2. **Processes and tools for project management**. Next, develop a project management methodology using some of the existing best practices and a standard framework, as explained in Chapter 5. At the same time, make sure that the application used for project management is adjusted to the methodology and is used effectively by all project managers. Allow one to two months for this phase.

3. **Processes and tools for project portfolio management**. The next step in the development process is to define the project selection and prioritization process and expand the roadmap. Choose the project portfolio management tool and opt for an out-of-the box or minimum-customization implementation. This process is one of the longest and could take up to four months, although it can be completed in three if the customization is kept to a minimum.

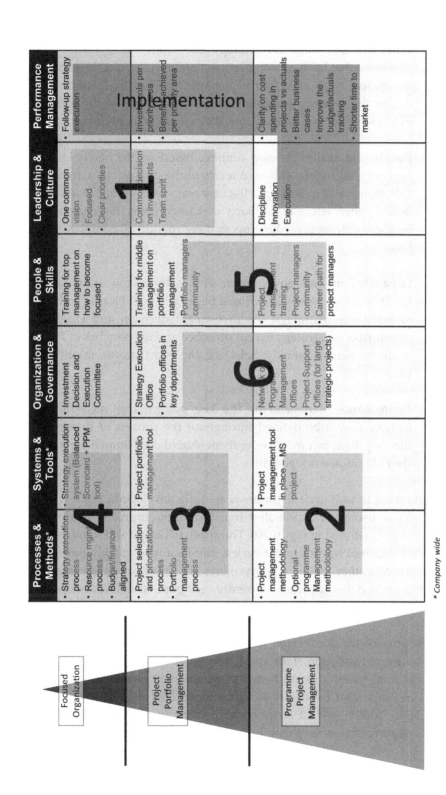

* Company wide

Figure 6.5   Maturity growth

4. **Processes and tools for strategy execution**. Next, identify the processes that have a strong connection with the run-the-business dimension, such as resource management and budgeting. Then define the strategy execution process and develop the strategy execution system. This step could take up to three months.

5. **People and skills**. Develop training based on the newly created processes and tools. Different levels of the organization, from top to bottom, need to be taught the new ways of working. In addition, define other HR aspects, such as career paths for change-the-business employees. Allow up to three months to complete these tasks.

6. **Organization and governance**. This activity can start earlier, but it is one of the most difficult because it will be met with lots of resistance. Although the investment decision and execution committee, the strategy execution office and the network of PMOs could be set up quickly, selecting the right people might take time.

7. **Performance management**. The key performance measurement metrics should be defined throughout the process of developing the six pillars, but monitoring them should start immediately after the new framework goes live.

It is important not to wait until all the areas are fully developed to start testing them. I propose using the accelerated transformation approach mentioned earlier, which is illustrated in Figure 6.6. The approach is fast and iterative and goes through different improvement cycles. The idea is to quickly develop a prototype and to gather further improvements directly from future users in the field. I have used this approach, currently very popular in IT development projects, for many years with large transformation projects.

The benefits of the accelerated transformation process include: a much shorter time frame; adoption starts much sooner; the solution better fits the needs of the final users; and the benefits are achieved much more quickly. Another very important benefit is that this accelerated way of running the transformation 'forces' project members to become focused, thus achieving high levels of performance for a long period.

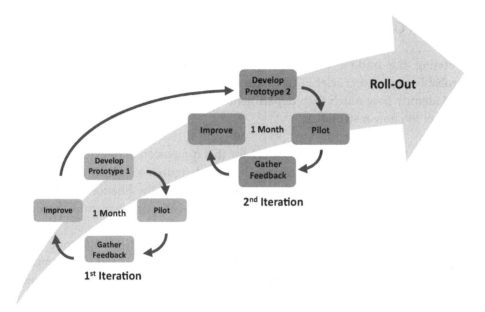

Figure 6.6   Accelerated transformation approach

Implement the Six-Pillar Framework

The rollout of the six pillars should follow the same sequence of steps as those used in their development, with testing of each area starting as soon as it is partially developed. The key stakeholders should be involved in these tests and should provide their input. With this approach, there is no clear-cut rollout phase; rather, the rollout starts just a few weeks after the maturity assessment has been completed.

The FOTP includes a few critical milestones, the successful and timely implementation of which strongly determines the project's success.

ADOPTION OF THE NEW PROCESSES

The adoption of the new processes has to be fast at every level of the organization. Project managers, for example, need to make sure that their projects follow the new guidelines and that the information is correctly included in the system. Management also needs to play its role with regard to the new processes, which means thoroughly understanding the projects and enforcing the use of the methodology to capture the new ideas. If management is not actively using the new tools and the new processes, the implementation will most probably fail.

LAUNCH OF THE FIRST DEDICATED BUDGET

Defining the budget dedicated to the change-the-business dimension is probably the most crucial FOTP milestone because it will bring transparency and identify how much each department spends. This process will also create most of the power struggles.

At first, because having a budget for this dimension is new, there will be neither accurate current figures nor historical figures to which they can be compared. The project manager, with the support of the finance department, will need to make assumptions to determine the most accurate picture of reality.

The most important component of achieving this critical milestone is an organization-wide change in mindset. Before becoming focused, departments had their own budgets and could decide in which projects to invest. Now, though, the change-the-business dimension has only one budget that finances all the initiatives for the entire organization. The decision about how to distribute this money is made by the investment decision and execution committee; and if a project is cancelled, the money goes back into the common pot. This sounds logical but, based on my experience, is one of the project's tipping points. Once the mindset changes from 'me' to 'we' a big step towards becoming a focused organization is taken.

ESTABLISHMENT OF THE STRATEGY EXECUTION OFFICE

The establishment of the strategy execution office, another key project milestone, should take place as soon as possible after the project has been launched. The SEO director,[3] appointed by top management, should have strong analytical skills, sound project management experience and excellent business knowledge. Communication and presentation skills are also essential as the SEO director will spend most of their time talking to key stakeholders from different levels in the organization.

The director's first task is to define the SEO's mission and vision and to set some measurable objectives for the years to come. It is important that these objectives are also ambitious and have a strong focus on excellence. The next step is to establish the office's operating model, which should include the following four sections:

---

3   In some organizations, the strategy execution office director could also be known as chief strategy execution officer.

- The SEO should become the source of all change-the-business (i.e., project-related) information,[4] including accurate data related to projects, budgets, actual expenditures, resources, capacity, forecasts, status of projects, risks, issues and so forth. In addition, the SEO should gather data about synergies realization by monitoring the business case and tracking the promised estimates in the business case. Last and most important, the SEO is responsible for providing top management with regular updates on how well the strategy is being executed and whether or not it is on track.

  The sooner the SEO director can regularly report this information, the faster the office will build credibility and be accepted as a key player in the organization. At the beginning, there will be gaps in the information and the quality of the data will be poor – appalling in some instances. However, starting with something imperfect and improving it over time is better than waiting until everything is perfect and risking not initiating the transformation at all.

- The office should include experienced managers who can understand the organization's projects and new ideas and who will serve as relationship managers. These experts will support all the organization's department heads and PMOs throughout the change and will coach them on how to implement the new processes and tools. This will help considerably in connecting the change-the-business with the run-the-business dimension.

  Another critical relationship management responsibility is to understand those projects that will be part of the roadmap. Relationship managers will need to be sufficiently familiar with the project content to be able to challenge projects that have issues or that do not make much sense.

  In addition, relationship managers play a very important role in helping the SEO director sell the new model to the organization. As mentioned earlier, some managers and several employees will resist this model and look for it to fail.

---

4   By information I do not mean data that can be extracted from the systems. Instead, I refer to the data that is analysed and synthesized so that management is able to make the best decisions.

- Besides the relationship managers, the SEO should have several brilliant project leaders. These project leaders will be in charge of the organization's most strategic cross-departmental projects, usually those that are the top priorities. They will have strong support from the CEO but will be under significant pressure to deliver.

- Finally, the SEO needs to have a section that is the keeper of all the methodologies, the processes and the tools related to the change-the-business dimension. This division will make sure that the documentation is up to date and that regular improvements are incorporated.

DEVELOPMENT OF THE STRATEGY EXECUTION SYSTEM

Another key milestone is the development and implementation of the strategy execution system. This system pulls together all the key data and then runs a simulation. The biggest issue is defining a common data model; that is, having a single companywide definition for each piece of data. Again, this is much easier said than done as companies have not paid too much attention to this issue and data has grown exponentially over the last decades.

Once the model is defined, the data has to be cleaned so that it achieves the highest level of accuracy. When the strategy execution system is ready, the organization can move to the final step of defining and agreeing on its first roadmap.

DELIVERY OF THE COMPANY'S FIRST STRATEGIC ROADMAP

Once the processes and the tools are in place, the final milestone is for the investment decision and execution committee to agree on which projects are a priority and to use that information to develop the company's first strategic roadmap. This is probably the most significant event in the entire transformation process.

Because everyone in the organization will be eager to hear the outcome of the first committee meeting, it is essential that the meeting is well prepared; that the information discussed is accurate; and that each committee member is carefully briefed in advance.

The committee will decide in which new ideas they will invest and which projects they will cancel or postpone and will then prioritize these elements and define the top projects. Together, members will agree on the roadmap for the years to come. Because the amount of information will be vast and the discussions could be unpredictable, I strongly recommend that most of the decisions be made before and not during this meeting. Taking this approach will avoid the possibility of a meeting where no decisions are made and top management fails to agree on a roadmap.

Another suggestion is to plan one or two additional committee meetings within the next two to three months so as to allow time for further discussions. Once the investment decision and execution committee has agreed on the prioritized roadmap, the company is ready to start executing the strategy.

Begin Executing the Strategy and Delivering the First Benefits

As soon as the six-pillar framework has been developed and the key milestones have been successfully implemented, the company is ready to become a focused organization. As shown in Figure 6.7, the benefits will start arriving with every step that is implemented. For example, once the leadership and culture step is implemented, the sense of urgency will be felt throughout the organization. The same applies to each of the improvement steps. At the end of the project, if every change has been completed successfully, the company will reach the status of focused organization.

The first financial benefits will start with the reduced number of projects and the associated budgetary savings. In addition, becoming focused creates a leaner change-the-business dimension, meaning that it is better organized and has fewer resources, especially external consultants.

Another big financial improvement is that the new selection system will allow management to stop investing in new projects without formal approval by the investment decision and execution committee. During its first few meetings, the committee will be presented with a huge number of ideas and projects seeking approval and funding. In the past, most of them would have been started, but now many are rejected, which represents significant savings.

The third financial benefit is that for the year to come there will already be fewer projects which have been more carefully selected and have strong support throughout their execution. This means faster implementation and delivery of the return on investment.

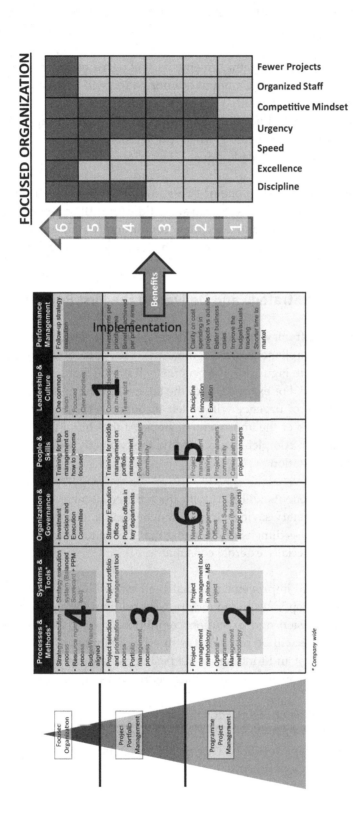

Figure 6.7   Benefits achieved

To start executing the strategy, it is important that all the elements described in the second part of the book are in place. The strategic roadmap will be the guide that will show the way through the years to come. It is up to top management to lead the organization through this path towards success.

Although painful, I do hope that your journey of becoming a focused organization is successful. I am sure that you and your employees will be proud and will enjoy the full benefits of being part of a focused organization.

Case Study: The Evolution of Spare Parts Benny, Inc.

Early Stages of Developing the Business

The year was 1913 and the global economy had begun to recover after a more than decade-long economic crisis. The public sector was pumping money into the economy like never before. Spare Parts Benny, Inc. – a spare parts production company founded three years prior by Benny White with loans of $600 – was booming.

Benny started his business in an old hut close to his home, with a team of five workers and one machine that produced spare parts – cylinders and valve gears – for the assembly of trains in the southwestern United States. Because the company was the first in the area to specialize in spare parts, Benny benefited from first-mover advantage. Benny was *extremely focused* on his business, determined to make it a success. He received many orders very quickly as there was a huge demand to reconstruct the country's infrastructure.

After only two years in the business, Spare Parts Benny, Inc. had more than 200 employees and five production machines. Concurrently, Benny began producing special parts for cars, at that time a new gadget for Americans. The first such vehicle, introduced by the Ford Motor Company on 1 October 1908, was called the Model T.

In the early 1910s, Benny White was one of the most successful businessmen in the country. Not only had he established six factories throughout the United States, employing more than 3,000 people, he was also selling his quality products to customers both in his country and abroad. His turnover had multiplied by 20 since he started his business, with consistent double-digit growth year after year. Benny's ambition was to become one of the largest spare parts producers in the world, a goal that was already within reach.

BUSINESS BOOM FOLLOWED BY DECLINE IN GROWTH

However in 1914, after four years of spectacular expansion, the business grew by only 9 per cent. Benny started to worry. That year, his company employed 5,000 people, 99 per cent of whom were operators who produced parts in the 11 factories across the country. The remaining employees included a team of six plant managers, a logistics manager and a sales manager, all of whom reported directly to Benny. Believing his managers to be largely unnecessary, Benny was the only person making decisions about the business.

MEETING WITH THE FATHER OF STANDARDIZATION – HENRY FORD

As business growth declined, Benny White turned to the academic world to learn new ways of running his business. At the time, no consulting companies existed – McKinsey was not founded until 1926 and the big accounting firms were in their early stages. So Benny sought the advice of one of his main customers, Henry Ford, who today is considered the father of standardization.[1]

Henry explained to Benny that in order to increase efficiency and reduce the number of employees, Ford Motor Company standardized its production processes and charged consistently low prices. Due to his huge success, Benny had become *unfocused*: in 1914 Spare Parts Benny, Inc. was producing 27 different types of components in each of its factories. Henry advised Benny to stop producing so many spare parts and instead to have each factory *focus* on producing a maximum of two items.

Ford explained to Benny that in order to be successful he first had to reduce prices, extend operations and finally improve the quality of his products. The first step – price reduction – had to be significant enough so that costs would be forced down. At the same time, Ford recommended that Benny pay his employees higher wages to keep them happy and motivated and to avoid high turnover. Ford's important final suggestion was that Benny increased the level of standardization by not giving his customers many choices. As he put it, 'Any customer can have a car painted any colour that he wants so long as it is black.'[2]

---

1   Henry Ford is considered the father of mass production. In 1913 he adopted the moving assembly line, having each worker doing one simple task in the production of the Model T. Henry Ford was also known for offering his workers a very generous daily wage – $5. By doing this he enabled many of them to buy the automobiles they made, thus helping the industry to expand.
2   Henry Ford (1922), *My Life and Work*, 72.

FIRST STRATEGIC PROJECT – STANDARDIZING THE PRODUCTION PROCESS

A few days later, Benny began a new improvement initiative – in fact, a strategic project – to standardize his company's production process and to reduce the number of spare parts produced. Benny developed a high-level plan, estimated the costs and made all the decisions without consulting the plant managers. He actually assumed, without knowing it, the role of project sponsor, project manager and steering committee, all at the same time. Of course these terms were never used and nor was the initiative called a project.[3]

In the mid-1910s, 'project management' did not exist either as a business term or as a management concept. Spare Parts Benny, Inc.'s initiative was expected to be completed after eight months of work for a total cost of $5,000. However, Benny found it difficult to manage the initiative in parallel with running the business, keeping existing customers happy and trying to expand the business into other markets.

After 10 months of work, the project had not achieved even half of Benny's objectives and costs were running out of hand. In addition, project delays and lack of project management created terrible consequences for the business. The quality of the spare parts fell, customers started to complain and workers threatened to go on strike because they did not understand the purpose of all of the changes. In fact, Benny had never fully briefed his management team or his employees about the standardization project. He was just giving them orders about what to change but never involved them in the decision making, which was the way businesses were run at the time.

MEETING WITH THE FATHER OF SCIENTIFIC MANAGEMENT – FREDERICK TAYLOR

Benny then realized that if he wanted to keep his business alive and finalize the project he needed some outside advice. In the winter of 1914 he arranged a meeting with Frederick Taylor, who is considered the father of scientific management. He drove his Model T alone[4] to the meeting at Harvard University,

---

3   Note that current terminology – e.g., words like project, project manager, project sponsor, programme manager, steering committee and so forth – were not yet used in the early to mid-1900s.

4   Benny did not take any member of his management team to visit Taylor – workshop sessions with so-called 'management gurus' is something that was only started almost half a century later.

which in 1908 was one of the first American universities to offer a graduate degree in business management – based on Taylor's principles. During his discussion with Benny, Taylor spoke extensively about the four principles of scientific management:[5]

1. Replace rule-of-thumb work methods with methods based on a scientific study of the tasks.

2. Scientifically select, train and develop each employee rather than passively leaving them to train themselves.

3. Provide detailed instructions and supervision of each worker in the performance of that worker's discrete task.

4. Divide work nearly equally between managers and workers so that the managers apply scientific management principles to planning the work and the workers actually perform the work.

Taylor also told Benny about the importance of examining his business with a bottom-up approach: start with the most elemental units of production process activity – the workers' actions; then study the effects of their actions on productivity and finally identify new methods for making these actions more efficient.

Benny was so enlightened by the discussion that before leaving Harvard University he bought six copies of Taylor's book *The Principles of Scientific Management* (1911), one for each of his managers. He had never before understood the importance of his management team so as soon as he was back at his headquarters, Benny called them into a meeting and asked them to read Taylor's book. At the same time, Benny decided to look again at his company's standardization initiative. After some analysis, he realized that he had not broken down the different production processes into their smallest components so it was difficult to determine with accuracy which step should be eliminated and which should be standardized. Following this brief reassessment, Benny relaunched the initiative and selected the head of engineering, Mike String, to be responsible for the mission.

The project began to run much more smoothly, with Benny *focused* on dealing with the most important business issues while Mike pushed the project

---

5   See Wikipedia at http://en.wikipedia.org/wiki/Frederick_Winslow_Taylor.

through. After 18 months, and at three times more than the estimated cost, the standardization project was complete. But Benny was happy with the result as these types of delays were usual in the business world – in fact they were the norm.

By the end of 1922, and thanks to Taylor's and Ford's advice, Spare Parts Benny, Inc. had reduced its number of products to nine, had closed two plants and had cut staff by 10 per cent while increasing the remaining staff's wages by 30 per cent. Benny started to see the benefits of Taylorism almost immediately after completing the initiative. He was producing goods faster at lower cost, so was able to sell more at a lower price.

The Great Depression

After the standardization project ended, Mike returned to work in business operations and no other large project or initiative was launched for at least a decade. Everybody in Spare Parts Benny, Inc. was working in operations, focusing on producing goods more efficiently and in larger quantities. Product quality improved, customer complaints diminished and employees returned to being content.

The business was doing so well that a financial advisor tried to pursuade Benny to sell part of his business and invest a portion of the proceeds in the stock market. Benny hesitated but ultimately decided to keep 100 per cent control of the business. This turned out to be an excellent decision because a year later, on 29 October 1929, the stock market experienced what today is known as the Great Crash (Black Thursday), the most devastating stock market collapse in the history of the United States.

The Great Crash led to the Great Depression, which became the longest, most widespread and deepest depression of the twentieth century. The timing of the Great Depression varied across nations, but in most countries it started in about 1929 and lasted until the late 1930s or early 1940s.

Spare Parts Benny, Inc., like most American businesses, was severely affected by the Great Depression. By June 1930, one-third of the company's orders had been cancelled, mainly those from US customers. With great regret, Benny had to lay off 1,000 of his 4,500 employees, most of whom had worked for him almost 15 years.

Additionally, the company was hit by the fact that 50 per cent of its sales were coming from abroad. When the economic crisis expanded internationally, exports dropped sharply, with a consequent loss in revenues for Spare Parts Benny, Inc. Over the next three years, 1,000 additional staff members had to be laid off.

Recovery from the Great Depression began in most countries in 1933, the common view among economic historians being that it ended with the advent of World War II. Government spending on the war caused double economic growth rates, ending most aspects of the crisis. America's entry into the war in 1941 finally eliminated the last effects of the Great Depression.

First Acquisition

Spare Parts Benny, Inc. survived the Great Depression by *focusing* on what had become its core business: producing spare parts for trains and cars. In February 1936, Benny received a visit from his banker, Simon Berkowitz, of Citizens and Southern Bank, whom he had met in 1910 shortly before starting his business. Simon was a cautious banker and had gained Benny's total trust: it was he who in 1928 had discouraged Benny from selling part of his business in order to invest in the stock market. This time, Simon's visit was to inform Benny that Aircraft Parts, Inc., one of the region's largest suppliers of components and materials to the aviation industry, was about to go bankrupt. Suggesting that this could be a great opportunity for Benny to expand his business, Simon showed him the papers from a light due diligence that he had completed on the company.

The economy was showing signs of recovery and it was an excellent moment to take some risks. Aircraft Parts had four plants across the US that employed a total of 1,350 people. Because of bad management, the company was in dire straits; thus, it would not require a large sum of money to be acquired. The benefits[6] for Spare Parts Benny could be substantial. Apart from the financial upside potential, Benny thought that after so many years of crisis and survival it could motivate his employees and boost their morale. With all of this in mind and on Simon's recommendation, he decided to go ahead with the acquisition. What Benny did not realize, however, was that this was going to be yet another strategic project.

6   At that time, the word 'synergy' did not exist as a business term, but was introduced as such by H. Igor Ansoff in his book *Corporate Strategy: An Analytic Approach to Business Policy for Growth and Expansion,* published in 1965.

After several months of negotiations, and with financing from Simon's bank, the deal was made. Benny decided that the merged companies would operate as one as of 1 January 1937 but when that date came nothing happened except for the name change from Spare Parts Benny, Inc. to Spare Parts 20th Century, Inc. The location of the company's headquarters remained the same. No changes were made either to the management team or to the organizational structure. Nobody was laid off. Both companies were run in parallel and worked exactly as they had previously, with one exception: Benny now spent a couple of days a week in the old Aircraft Parts, Inc. facilities. Nobody had told Benny that an acquisition is a project and that both businesses had to be integrated in order to obtain the expected benefits.

This situation continued for several years. Benny was de facto running two companies, travelling once a week to the acquired business and spending most of his time at work. His main priority was to improve the Aircraft Parts business; consequently, Benny rarely saw his family.

Knowing that this situation had to change, Benny applied Ford's and Taylor's advice as well as the knowledge gained from the Spare Parts Benny standardization initiative to making significant changes to Aircraft Parts, Inc. He discontinued production of five of 12 parts and focused primarily on manufacturing brakes – stators and rotors. This time, Benny chose a supervisor[7] to carry out the changes in the four plants he had acquired and maintained a distance from him – mainly because he needed time to run his other business – that proved beneficial. He also developed a more realistic plan and budget.

Without realizing it, Benny was acting as the project sponsor, monitoring progress bi-weekly and making decisions whenever necessary. This standardization project lasted only 10 months (eight months less than the one at Spare Parts Benny, Inc.), and the budget overrun was only twice the original estimate (instead of triple 23 years earlier). At the time, this was one of the best executed projects in the industry.

Sales picked up quickly, and Spare Parts 20th Century began growing by double digits. Much of that growth came from government contracts. In 1939, World War II had just started and demands from governments for huge amounts of heavy machinery, including aeroplanes and armoured cars, benefited the company enormously.

---

7   As stated earlier, in the 1930s, the term 'project manager' was not yet used.

The Impact of World War II

The Ford Motor Company continued to be Spare Parts 20th Century's biggest client. As Ford's successes grew, so did the demand for spare car parts. Ford was opening plants in Britain, Canada, Italy, Australia, India and France; and soon after, Benny was receiving orders from these countries. Benny's old management style, typical of the times, demanded that he be onsite all the time; and he had never considered opening plants abroad or taken the time to develop a vision or strategy for his business.

In the 1930s and early 1940s, Spare Parts 20th Century specialized in producing spare parts for war cars, especially for the American M8 Light Armored Car – a 6×6 vehicle produced by the Ford Motor Company.

During World War II, Ford had expanded into the aviation business with the production of Liberty engines. According to economists, the company played a pivotal role in the Allied victory. With Europe under siege, Ford turned to mass production for the war effort. Specifically, Ford mass produced the B-24 Liberator bomber,[8] still the most produced Allied bomber in history. When these planes were deployed in the war zones, the balance of power shifted to the Allies.

Benny benefited largely from Ford's success in the aviation industry. The acquisition of Aircraft Parts also became one his best decisions time-wise. This part of the business also grew exponentially, and the fact that the standardization project concluded right on time allowed Benny to produce the best spare parts for the B-24 Liberator bomber.

In 1945, eight years after Spare Parts Benny, Inc. acquired Aircraft Parts, Inc., the companies were still not integrated. Both companies grew extremely fast and became very successful but, apart from the name change and the standardization project, nothing was done to combine them. Responding to their rapid growth, both companies had enlarged their management teams. They also had created two separate sales and logistics departments. Consequently, overhead costs were growing at the same pace as revenues.

---

8   Before Ford, and under optimal conditions, the aviation industry could produce one
    Consolidated Aircraft B-24 bomber a day at an aircraft plant. Ford showed the world how
    to produce one B-24 an hour at a peak of 600 per month in 24-hour shifts. Ford's Willow Run
    factory broke ground in April 1941. At the time, it was the largest assembly plant in the world,
    with more than 3,500,000 square feet (330,000 m^2). Source: Wikipedia.

Benny had been keeping the books for Spare Parts 20th Century since the beginning, but managing the growth of what remained essentially two companies left him with little time for dealing with their finances. He went to Citizens and Southern Bank and consulted his banker, Simon, who advised him to hire one person to be responsible for all the finances for the merged companies. At first Benny hesitated, since he alone had always controlled his companies' money and he felt that letting go of this part of the business was a huge risk. On the other hand, Simon had made some excellent recommendations in the past and when he suggested that one of his colleagues, Michael Clark, assume the position of manager of finances and accounting, Benny immediately hired him. Once again, this decision proved to be the right one. Michael was good at his work and very quickly gained Benny's trust. Benny benefited enormously from this change, first because he now had more time to grow his business and second because he had a better overview of the new company's finances.

Meeting with the First Management Consultant – Peter Drucker

In 1946, shortly after hiring Michael to manage Spare Parts 20th Century's finances, Benny had the pleasure of meeting Peter Drucker, who at that time was teaching at Bennington College. Later, he taught at New York University and Claremont Graduate School, where he developed one of the first executive MBA programmes for working professionals. In addition to teaching, Peter was one of the most renowned management consultants in the US. From 1943 until 1945, he had worked with the board members and the executive team of General Motors, which at the time was one of the largest companies in the world. Peter's work resulted in a book that had just been released.[9]

Benny had a very interesting chat with Peter, describing the genesis of Spare Parts Benny, Inc.; his encounters with Ford and Taylor; the acquisition of Aviation Parts, Inc.; and his coaching on how to manage 'short-term assignments' while running the business – at that time, the terms 'projects' and 'project management' were still unknown.

Peter was curious to find out from Benny why Spare Parts Benny, Inc. and Aviation Parts, Inc. had not yet been integrated. He told Benny that the two businesses were missing a big opportunity to reduce costs and consolidate their back office activities. Peter's first impression was that Spare Parts 20th Century had developed the basic manufacturing efficiencies and managerial

---

9   Peter Drucker (1946), *Concept of the Corporation.*

hierarchies of mass production. In addition, although Benny clearly knew how to run his business, Peter told Benny that now was the time for him to bring his company to a higher level by moving from the command-and-control management model to a more decentralized organization.

Peter explained that his central business philosophy pertained to respecting the workers; he strongly believed that people were a company's most valuable resource and that a manager's job was to prepare them to perform. In addition, Peter revealed that he was developing a new business method called 'management by objectives,'[10] which involved managing business by balancing a variety of needs and goals.

After his discussion with Peter, Benny was both confused and enlightened. He was astonished that he had missed so many important aspects of managing a business which after talking to Peter were so obvious. Peter encouraged Benny by suggesting that he use the integration of the two businesses as an opportunity to make some fundamental changes. At the end of their conversation, Benny promised to keep Peter informed about the progress of Spare Parts 20th Century.

Integrating and Decentralizing Spare Parts 20th Century

Benny was very happy with the knowledge he had acquired from these brilliant 'management gurus' and the more he thought about their ideas, the better he recognized their benefits. At the time, very few business owners would have sought outside advice; but Benny was different. The day after his conversation with Peter Drucker, Benny convened an urgent meeting of his entire management team. Strangely enough, this was the first time that managers from the two entities had sat together since the merger was announced more than nine years earlier. Benny spoke about his conversation with Peter Drucker and of his decision to make two very important changes to his business:

- Integration – the creation of a single company.

- Decentralization – empowerment of management and staff.

Benny appointed Michael Clark, his chief financial officer (CFO) – at that time the concept of programme manager also did not exist – as coordinator of these

---

10 This concept was later detailed in his book *The Practice of Management*, published in 1954.

two initiatives. Each initiative had a separate leader, with integration being led by a plant manager named Bob McCain (who was nearing retirement), while the head of decentralization was another senior plant manager, Stuart Miles.

Both initiatives were launched in the summer of 1947. There was an initial meeting[11] between Benny, Michael, Bob and Stuart, during which they discussed and agreed on the main objectives. The intention was to have both initiatives completed in ten months, by April 1948. Benny was not entirely pleased with this target completion date because he felt that the tasks were simple and should require a maximum of six months. However, his previous experiences with changes in the company taught him to be cautious.

Neither Stuart nor Bob was fully dedicated to executing his respective initiative, as each was still responsible for his day-to-day management functions. Michael was totally focused on the finances of the company, which meant that he did not have time to coordinate and follow up on the initiatives' progress.

The first signs of trouble came in December 1947, only five months after launching the two strategic initiatives, when it became obvious that no real progress had been made and that the only deliverables were ideas.

Bob's biggest contribution to the integration project was his proposal that the management team move into the old Spare Parts Benny headquarters. He was convinced that this move alone would almost complete the integration initiative. Bob's work did not involve a thorough assessment of whether the entire management team could reside in one location; nor did he mobilize other people within the company. Instead, he just casually mentioned to some of his colleagues that they would soon be changing offices. In fairness, however, Bob was very busy with running his plant's day-to-day operations.

On the other hand, Stuart began his leadership of the decentralization initiative by setting up a team of experts – mainly plant managers and sales force members – from different areas of the business. He held a meeting at which all the team members were able to share their views on how to complete the decentralization.[12] One of the suggestions was to create a thin management layer which would be located in a site smaller than the existing one, but that was brand new. Another proposal was to have three business units: the first

---

11   In 1947, the term 'project kickoff' did not yet exist.
12   'Workshop' and 'brainstorming' were not terms used in 1947.

focusing on car spare parts; the second on train spare parts; and the third on aircraft spare parts. Each business unit would have its own management group that reported to the central team.

The decentralization initiative produced revolutionary ideas, and Stuart was proud of the outcome of his work. However, when he shared these ideas with management they did not like the thought of changing the location and structure of the company.

The person with overall responsibility[13] for the two initiatives, Michael Clark, had not been involved in any meetings other than the initial one with Benny, Bob and Stuart. This was because he had no free time, since all his efforts went into dealing with Spare Parts 20th Century's finances. During the five months since the launch of the initiatives, Benny had asked Michael how they were going and received the response: 'You have nothing to worry about, Benny; we are on a roll.'

After seeing no real progress and hearing rumours that some employees were against the change, Benny started to worry. A few years prior he would have gone directly to Bob and Stuart to find out what was going on. But he chose to implement Peter Drucker's advice to empower employees by allowing Michael to head the initiatives and maintaining contact solely with him.

After one more month with no visible progress and signs of management resistance to changing locations, Benny called a meeting with his three initiative leaders. What struck him right away was that neither Bob nor Stuart had discussed with each other their respective ideas and progress. They were both embarrassed when they realized that they had come up with completely opposite proposals. Michael looked totally lost and Benny could not hide his disappointment or his concern about the rumours that some managers were against any change. Once again, like some years ago, a temporary endeavour had become something difficult to manage and execute. Benny said that he needed two days to think about why this total misalignment happened and ordered Bob and Stuart to put their initiatives on hold until then.

After careful consideration of why all of these problems and misalignments were happening, Benny reached two important conclusions:

---

13 Note that current terminology – e.g., words like projects, project manager, project sponsor, programme manager, steering committee and so forth – was not yet used in the 1940s and 1950s.

1.   This was the first time that the company was running two important change initiatives simultaneously, therefore lack of coordination between initiatives and two different leadership styles had created opposing ideas and confusion within Benny's management team.

2.   These two initiatives differed from previous ones in that they strongly affected all the company's employees. For reasons that Benny did not fully understand yet, initiatives that heavily involved workers were more difficult to implement.

Benny concluded that his company was not mature enough to absorb two significant changes simultaneously. He therefore decided to postpone the decentralization initiative and to go forward with the integration. Stuart was put in charge of that initiative, reporting directly to Benny. Bob and Michael were released from these special tasks and went back to their usual jobs full time.

Stuart was asked to lead the decentralization initiative because Benny was impressed with his innovative decision to involve different experts. Under normal circumstances Benny would have given the job to Bob, who was much older and more experienced than Stuart and used to the top-down approach. However, Benny wanted to see 21-year-old Stuart in action.

The first thing Stuart did was organize a meeting with senior managers from both Spare Parts Benny and Aviation Parts. He invited 12 colleagues from different plants, but only seven showed up. Stuart was amazed to see that ten years after the acquisition, both companies still had little in common besides the new name.

In this first meeting Stuart received anxious questions from most of the attendees, such as 'Why should we change if we are doing fine?' and 'How is this going to impact my situation?' They did not seem to be supportive of the integration initiative and they were frustrated because they were not in control. Stuart was not expecting this response. He decided to end the meeting without any clear conclusions but to schedule a second meeting for the following week.

Stuart then decided to do something different. He convinced Benny that he needed to be at the second meeting. Stuart felt that in order for the integration initiative to work, it was critical that the head of the company show his support.

Although Benny was not used to large meetings and did not understand right away why he needed to attend, he accepted the invitation. On the day of the second meeting all 12 managers were present and on time. Stuart began the proceedings by thanking Benny for attending and restating the objectives of the integration initiative. This time no one expressed any opinions or shared any concerns and, most surprisingly, everybody agreed that integration was necessary. The managers decided that they would develop a plan to present to Benny in three months, just before summer.

Stuart was amazed to see the difference between the first and the second meeting. Although he was certain that Benny's presence had made a big difference, he believed that something else had contributed to the shift as well.

One month later, on 7 April 1947, Henry Ford died at the age of 83. That was a very sad day for Benny. Not only had Ford's company been Spare Parts Benny's only major customer for decades, but Ford himself had also been Benny's business mentor.

Toward the end of 1948 the integration of Spare Parts Benny, Inc. and Aviation Parts, Inc. was complete. A new head office was established and some functions were centralized, such as capacity planning and shipping. The team proposed the creation of two additional departments, one in charge of coordinating the sales activities and a second one to manage client product returns. Each plant would have someone responsible for finances who would report to Michael Clark, the finance director located in the main office.

One result of the integration was that expenses were reduced: two plants were closed without affecting overall production as the work had been shifted to other plants in the group. Also, despite the integration, Spare Parts 20th Century's business continued to boom. Sales had tripled since 1943, reaching a historic high of $1,573,000; and the number of staff grew, reaching 8,450. Apart from the few people working on the new change initiatives, the rest of the employees in the company were working on operational tasks.

Benny, the New Tycoon – BeWhite Corporation

During the following years Benny saw his company expand exponentially. Thanks to the successful integration of the two businesses, and booming sales, Spare Parts 20th Century was extremely cash rich. Benny's fear that the end of

World War II would have a negative effect on the economy and would bring back the difficult times of the Great Depression never materialized.

In addition to having a cash surplus, Benny – pushed by Peter Drucker's teachings about the 'knowledge worker' – had begun to empower his management team and was reaping the benefits. Because he had delegated some of his day-to-day tasks to them, Benny now had more time to think about how to expand his business. He also wanted to further leverage the learning he had acquired in the past 40 years. Benny sought the advice of his old friend Simon Berkowitz, who had recently been appointed branch director of LaSalle Bank, on where to invest his company's extra money. Benny was not too keen to invest in the stock market and was more interested in buying additional businesses, as his previous purchase had been very successful. Simon advised him to diversify and to invest in other industries, stating specifically that: 'Diversification would reduce your investment risk. For example, if the market for spare train parts collapsed, this could be counterbalanced by growth in another division, for instance, aircraft spare parts. This advantage is enhanced by the fact that the business cycle affects industries in different ways.' As usual, Benny was impressed and enlightened by the words of his old friend. He decided to follow Simon's advice and, without realizing it at the time, initiated one of the largest conglomerates in the United States in the second half of the twentieth century.

After some research, Benny decided to acquire Cementex, Inc., a small construction company that was not performing too well. Benny was convinced that he could use his experience to multiply the company's revenues by five in less than three years. Negotiations with the owner began in early 1952 and proceeded quickly, since Benny paid a fair amount of money and offered the former owner a position in the new company.

This time, Benny gathered all his management team to announce the deal. Because he now realized the benefits of keeping his direct reports informed, Benny had four management meetings per year – as opposed to almost none in the previous 40 years. He asked Stuart Miles to integrate this newly acquired business and to come up with a name that would better suit the new company.

Despite now being 60 years old, Benny had the same energy, passion and excitement that he had experienced during his first years in business. His oldest son, Paul White, had joined Spare Parts 20th Century one year earlier after obtaining an MBA from the American Institute for Foreign Trade (better known as Thunderbird School of Global Management), the oldest business school specializing in international management.[14] Paul had the same passion for business management as his father; in fact, he received the Barton Kyle Yount Award for best student in his graduating class. Benny asked his son to work with Stuart Miles on the integration of Cementex.

Stuart began Cementex's integration with Paul White's support. Once again he organized several meetings with Benny and the management team from the old and new businesses. Because these meetings were held in an old plant room where manual work had been performed, Stuart called them 'workshops.' The workshops were a very useful way for attendees to exchange information. It was decided that the best way to integrate Cementex was to create a holding company; to keep a decentralized model (as Peter Drucker had suggested six years earlier); and to integrate such back office activities as logistics and finance. The new company was called 'Constructions Benny' and the holding company was named 'BeWhite Corporation.'

Paul White suggested to Stuart that he show the project's schedule and progress in visual form using a Gantt chart,[15] a tool that Paul had learned about during his MBA studies. Stuart, always curious about new ways to more efficiently complete a job, bought the idea straight away. During the next workshop, Stuart displayed a Gantt chart that illustrated the integration plan with task bars and milestones and outlined the sequence and duration of all tasks in a process. Benny was astonished that the chart helped him understand the plan quickly and, recognizing that it was a powerful analytical tool, Benny asked Stuart to provide him with an updated version of the Gantt chart every month.

The integration of Cementex was the most successful project in the history of the company, lasting less than nine months and just doubling the initial cost estimates. Nobody discussed or asked to be shown any quantifiable benefits of the project, but this was normal during those days.[16]

---

14   Thunderbird School of Global Management was founded in 1946 by Lieutenant General Barton Kyle Yount, the Commanding General of the US Army Air Training Command.

15   The Gantt chart was developed during the first decade of the 1900s by Henry L. Gantt (1861–1919), a mechanical engineer and management consultant. Gantt worked directly with Frederick W. Taylor as an associate, using scientific management principles to increase productivity. The Gantt chart was based on Gantt's work in the shipbuilding industry during World War I. Officially, the chart was used to schedule and monitor large construction projects like the Hoover Dam, which started in 1931, or the Eisenhower highway network launched in 1956. This chart is the forerunner to many modern project management tools, including the work breakdown structure (WBS) and resource allocation.

16   'Benefits management' as a concept that indicates how to capture and report on the achievements of the original benefits of a project was introduced only in the late 1990s.

Benny appointed his son Paul as chief executive of Constructions Benny and this new company very quickly became another big success. Originally, Cementex was building homes in the southern US. Within a few years, however, Paul had used his knowledge to develop one of the most successful diversified building companies in the United States, with services ranging from construction contracting and industrial construction to infrastructure, new home construction and manufactured housing. Paul understood the cyclical nature of the construction industry, so he protected the business not only through diversification but also through geographical expansion outside the United States. Thanks to the international expansion, Constructions Benny benefited largely from the economic aid that flowed to European countries under the Marshall Plan.[17]

The old business, Spare Parts 20th Century, also had extremely wealthy years after the war. The automobile industry successfully returned to producing cars, and aviation became an important industry for civilians as well as for the military. In addition, the need to produce war supplies had given rise to a huge military-industrial complex, and spending did not disappear with the war's end. On the contrary, the Iron Curtain descended across Europe and the United States found itself embroiled in a cold war with the Soviet Union. Consequently, the government maintained substantial spending in the industry, from which Spare Parts 20th Century greatly benefited.

By the end of the 1950s, Benny had acquired three additional businesses: C-Transistors, an electronics company with 12,300 employees specialized in bipolar junction transistors for second-generation computers; Medical Labs, a pharmaceutical company with 27,100 employees specialized in antibiotic drugs that had gone public in 1953; and YourMoney, a financial services company with 21,900 employees specialized in commercial banking for small and medium-sized enterprises. Once again, Stuart successfully integrated all three of these companies, although this time Benny decided to retain their original names to keep their established brand equity and brand recognition. BeWhite Corporation became one of the largest conglomerates in the United States. In

---

17 Marshall Plan aid was used mainly for the purchase of goods from the United States but also contributed to the financing of war-ravaged infrastructures. Between 1948 and 1951 the United States poured financial aid totalling $13 billion (about $100 billion at 2003 prices) into the economies of Western Europe. Officially termed the European Recovery Program (ERP), the Marshall Plan was approved by Congress in the Economic Cooperation Act of April 1948. The Marshall Plan spanned three ERP years from July 1948 to June 1951. General Marshall was awarded the Nobel Peace Prize in 1953 for his role as architect and advocate of the Marshall Plan.

1959, with gross revenues of $2,169.4 million and more than 80,000 employees, BeWhite Corporation reached number 11 in the year's *Fortune* 500 listing, just below giant AT&T Technologies and above Chrysler.

After 50 years of hard work, Benny had become one the tycoons of the business world. But, as opposed to many of the other tycoons, Benny had built his empire by having a sharp eye for business opportunities; listening to the advice of trusted experts; introducing improvements in his management method; and empowering his management team, which was unusual at that time.

Meeting with the Father of Strategy Management – Igor Ansoff

During the first half of the 1960s, the BeWhite Corporation continued to grow and expand internationally. Most of the individual businesses were successful, with Constructions Benny booming. But Spare Parts 20th Century started to decline. Benny did not have the same energy as he felt during the early years and he began to delegate more of his management work to his son Paul, who carried on his father's legacy of enthusiasm and business acumen.

However, with the diversification into other industries, Benny started to lose sight of all that was happening in BeWhite Corporation. Managing each of the unrelated businesses equally well turned out to be a challenge. The five different businesses that were part of the conglomerate put extra layers between Benny and the people in the factories, which in turn increased management costs. The complexity of Benny's empire was also reflected in the finances. Michael Clark, the CFO, had difficulty providing Benny with a consolidated overview of the financial health of the BeWhite Corporation and was not able to easily explain the financial makeup of the individual businesses. In addition, Benny started to hear of disputes among some managers. This was unthinkable 10 years earlier, when fellowship was one of the key values across all the businesses, starting with Benny and his management team. Benny also noticed that every year his businesses had more short-term assignments with specific goals – such as the building of a new plant in a foreign country – but he did not have a clear overview of these assignments either.

One morning in April 1966, Benny and his son Paul had a long discussion to try to take stock of the situation. They agreed that the diversification begun in 1952 had proved to be an excellent decision but that the incredible growth of the past years had caused them to *lose focus* and control of the company. Paul used his network built during his years at business school to organize a meeting with Igor Ansoff, a Russian emigrant who had been teaching at United States International University[18] and who was considered the father of strategic management. Igor was an instructor in physics at the US Naval Academy during World War II, where he developed some of his theories and concepts.[19]

As in the good old days, Benny drove his brand-new Ford – this one a Galaxie Sunliner[20] – to Carnegie Mellon University in Pittsburgh, Pennsylvania, where Igor Ansoff was Professor of Industrial Administration. Igor welcomed Benny and Paul warmly into his office as by then Benny was one of the most respected personalities in the United States, due to his business success and humble management style.

Igor explained that with increased competition, greater interest in acquisitions and diversification – concepts well known to Benny and Paul – and a quickly changing business environment, business leaders could no longer ignore strategic issues. He stressed that when Benny and his management team developed BeWhite Corporation's strategy, it was essential to anticipate possible future environmental challenges and draw up appropriate strategic plans for responding to these challenges. Igor often cited examples from his years in the US Army. He described in detail his new classification method of decision making, the famous '3S model':[21]

- **Strategy** – related to areas of products and markets.

- **Structure** – related to administrative areas (organizational and resource allocating).

- **Systems** – related to operational areas (budgeting and directly managing).

---

18 Today known as Alliant International University, in San Diego, California.
19 Many of the current business and strategic planning terms, such as Mission, Vision, SWOT and so forth were developed by the army during wartime in the second half of the nineteenth century and the first half of the twentieth century, when these methods were applied to management and marketing.
20 Ford Motor Company ceased production of the Model T on 26 May 1927. As a tribute to his mentor, Henry Ford, Benny White drove Ford cars his entire life.
21 To some extent, he based himself on Alfred Chandler's work *Strategy and Structure* (1962). The 3S model was later developed into the 7S model by the strategy consulting firm McKinsey.

'Strategy decisions are different because they always apply to new situations and so need to be made anew every time,' concluded Igor, who then proceeded to explain that to establish a link between past and future corporate activities[22] four key strategy components should be defined:

- *Product-market scope*: a clear idea of what products a business is responsible for.

- *Growth vector*: a way of exploring how growth might be achieved in the future.

- *Competitive advantage*: competencies a company possesses that will enable it to compete effectively. Every company should build its business around a core capability,[23] skill or knowledge in which it excels and through which it can beat the competition.

- *Synergy*: Igor explained the term synergy as '2 + 2 = 5,' or how the whole is greater than the mere sum of the parts, and that it required an analysis of how new opportunities fit within the core capabilities of the business.

During the final part of the meeting Igor explained his 'Product-Market Growth Matrix,' a 2 × 2 matrix created to assess different strategies to grow a business via existing or new products, in either existing or new markets. Of the four strategic options given in the matrix:

- *Market penetration* means increasing existing product market share in existing served markets.

- *Market expansion* means the identification of new customers for existing products.

- *Product expansion* means developing new products for existing customers.

- *Diversification* requires new products to be produced for new markets.

---

22 Ansoff formulated the well-known 'Gap analysis,' which is the comparison between actual and potential performance and its objectives.
23 Ansoff's concept of core capability was later adopted and expanded by Prahalad and Hamel in their 1990 *Harvard Business Review* article, The core competence of a corporation.

Benny was once again fascinated by the clarity and simplicity of Igor's concepts, a common characteristic of the other management gurus he had met in the past. He imagined that if he had not become a business person, he would have liked to have become a management thinker like them and write books about his theories. Benny also wondered how it was possible that companies had managed to be successful for so many decades without thinking too much about strategic issues. BeWhite Corporation had been applying a traditional planning method based on an extended budgeting system that took the annual budget and then projected it three years into the future. Paul confirmed that this approach did not pay too much attention to strategic issues. Benny bought several copies of Igor's just released book *Corporate Strategy* and agreed to keep in touch.

At the next quarterly management meeting in the spring of 1965, Benny shared Igor Ansoff's theories and methods. He asked the chief executives of all five businesses to look into strategic issues and potential changes in the environment they might be facing in the future and to use the 3S model and Ansoff matrix to facilitate this analysis. At the end of this process, Benny expected a strategic plan for each of the five businesses.

For the first time in his life, Benny hired a so-called 'business consultant,' his son Paul's MBA classmate and good friend who two years earlier, in 1963, had founded The Boston Consulting Group (BCG). The consultant would assist the management team in this first strategic exercise, the results of which would be presented during the next quarterly management meeting in the summer.

The Birth of Project Management as a Profession

In the meantime, Stuart and Paul continued their search for new management techniques and tools to handle their growth in a quickly changing and competitive world. Their main focus was on improving the short-term assignments that were so different from the day-to-day activities of running the businesses. They had been very successful in applying the Gantt chart to all the initiatives, and the improvements in terms of common understanding and reduction of delays had been significant. Paul, through his role as chief executive of Constructions Benny, encouraged his managers to look for new techniques to improve the way these initiatives were carried out. Paul soon realized that the construction business was based purely on short-term assignments with limited budgets and resources.[24] The US government, the construction industry's main client, also mandated the use of certain methods and tools to improve the way projects where controlled.

While attending a two-day alumni seminar at Thunderbird about the US Navy Polaris nuclear submarine project, Paul learned about the Project Evaluation and Review Technique (commonly known as the PERT method). In 1957, the Navy Special Projects Office developed this technique to analyse the time needed to complete each task in a project in order to identify the minimum time needed to finish the total project. The main goal was to simplify the planning and scheduling of large and complex projects.

At the seminar, Paul met James Kelly and Morgan Walker, who in 1959 had published the first article on the Critical Path Method (CPM), a new project management modelling technique similar to the PERT method.[25] Morgan explained to Paul that: 'CPM is a technique used to calculate the longest path to the end of the project. It looks at the earliest and latest that each activity can start and finish without having an impact on the total length of the project.' Anticipating a question from Paul, James continued by saying: 'The main difference between PERT and CPM is that PERT focuses on time as the key variable, while CPM focuses on the critical activities to complete the project.' Paul thanked James and Morgan and invited them to share their views with the Constructions Benny management team.

As soon as Paul was back in his office, he explained to Stuart what he had learned in the seminar. Stuart was as enthusiastic as Paul, and both were anxious to test the new methods. After conducting a training session on the CPM and PERT methods, Paul asked his management team to use both methods for each new initiative to estimate the duration and end date of the projects. The outcome was to be presented in one Gantt chart per project.

One month later, the managers had done their work and the outcome was spectacular. Never before Paul had such a clear overview of all the projects Constructions Benny was working on, including when they would be completed.[26] He decided to present the outcome to his management team at the

---

24 Construction is a project-based industry; most of the business and core activities are carried out via projects.
25 E.J. Kelly and M.R. Walker, Critical Path Planning and Scheduling, Proceedings of the Eastern Joint Computer Conference, Boston, MA, March 1959.
26 It is important to note that this overview showed no association between the different projects and the company's strategy.

next quarterly meeting. At the meeting, in the summer of 1965, the five chief executives presented their strategic plans and product growth matrices using transparencies and a 3M 1720 black and white overhead projector.[27] These illustrations clearly showed the differences between the businesses and their markets and led the management team to adopt the following strategies:

- *Spare Parts 20th Century* = Increase market share in the automotive and trains spare parts markets and look for new products in the aviation sector (market penetration and expansion).

- *Constructions Benny* = Identify new customers for the different products and services that are already offered successfully (market expansion).

- *C-Transistors* = Increase market share for transistors in the developing computer market (market penetration).

- *Medical Labs* = Increase market share for antibiotic drugs and research additional drugs with which to enter new markets (market penetration and diversification).

- *YourMoney* = Develop investment banking products with which to enter new markets (diversification).

The meeting concluded with Paul's presentation on PERT and CPM, his new management techniques for projects. Some executives found it a bit complicated and mentioned that they preferred the Gantt charts. Overall, Benny was very pleased with the outcome of the meeting[28] and impressed by the willingness of his management team to use the new management techniques he was proposing – unaware that this was due to his leadership and management style.

A few months later, Stuart Miles and Paul White flew to Vienna to participate in a forum for European network planning practitioners to exchange knowledge and experiences on project scheduling. Both of them were considered experts in the area of project management. Stuart recalled some years later that,

---

27 PowerPoint did not exist at that time. The first version – called Presenter – was developed in 1984 by Forethought, Inc., a start-up that Microsoft acquired three years later. The first version of the software under the Microsoft banner was released for Windows 3.0 in 1990.

28 It is important to note that none of the five strategic plans was actually linked to any project. With Paul's exercise the opposite happened: the projects were not linked to any strategic objective but no one noticed this flaw, not even Benny or the BCG business consultant.

ironically, *'during this sessions everybody was talking about scheduling and network analysis, nothing else, and the phrase 'project management' was just not used at all.'* This forum led to the creation, in 1972, of the International Management Systems Association (IMSA), renamed the International Project Management Association (IPMA) in 1979.[29]

In 1969, Paul and Stuart, along with eight other project management experts, were invited to a gathering in Philadelphia. Of the 10 attendees, most – for example, Jim Snyder, Russell D. Archibald, J. Gordon Davies, E.A. 'Ned' Engman, Eric Jenett and Susan Gallagher – were skilled in CPM and PERT techniques. This gathering led to the creation of the Project Management Institute (PMI),[30] a not-for-profit organization formed to serve the interests of the project management industry. A key shared belief among these experts, including Paul and Stuart, was that the tools and techniques of project management were the same even among the widespread application of projects, from the automobile to the construction industry.

In 1984, the PMI began offering a professional certification (Project Management Professional, or PMP) for those who wanted to be recognized in the profession. Another major achievement of the PMI was the introduction in 1987 of *A Guide to the Project Management Body of Knowledge* (referred to as the *PMBOK® Guide*), which describes all of the project management techniques and best practices to help keep them clear and consistent.

BeWhite Corporation Goes Public and Suffers a Loss

Good results continued for BeWhite Corporation during the final years of the 1960s and the early part of the 1970s. All five businesses increased their revenues and expanded internationally, although at the same time costs and expenses were escalating. In addition, the excess cash in the bank was diminishing rapidly: each business had many ideas to invest in and, due to strong decentralization, CFO Michael Clark had little control of the financial situation. Another warning sign was that despite having spent several weeks and paid BCG a couple of thousand dollars to help on the strategic exercise, the strategic plans were untouched. No one took care of following them up.

---

29 Today IPMA has become a federation of around 45 project management associations with more than 40,000 members.
30 Today, the PMI has 500,000 members, including 370,000 PMP-accredited practitioners in more than 185 countries.

The US government increased its military spending with the war in Vietnam, which benefited Spare Parts 20th Century in the short term. Federal spending on health care (Medicare) also increased dramatically, which greatly benefited Medical Labs sales. At the end of the 1960s, however, the government's failure to raise taxes to pay for these efforts led to accelerating inflation, which eroded this prosperity. The 1973–74 oil embargo by members of the Organization of Petroleum Exporting Countries (OPEC) rapidly pushed energy prices higher and created shortages. Even after the embargo, energy prices stayed high, adding to inflation and eventually causing rising rates of unemployment. Federal budget deficits grew, foreign competition intensified and the stock market sagged.

In the meantime, a very good friend of Paul had insisted that he meet Charles Francis Morgan, son of Henry Morgan, an American banker who in 1935 had co-founded the financial institution Morgan Stanley. Charles was trying to persuade Paul to go public with BeWhite Corporation. He explained many times the benefits of being quoted on Wall Street, the most important being that BeWhite Corporation would be able to raise money for future growth plans. Charles also pointed out that Benny and Paul could cash in, which could make them and their management and employees very rich.

Paul discussed the initial public offering (IPO) possibility with Benny, who was not opposed to the idea as many of his competitors had recently gone public too. On the other hand, Benny's old friend and former banker Simon Berkowitz, who had recently been recruited by Chase Manhattan to head the consumer retail division, was totally against it. Simon mentioned some the risks of being a public company, which included:

- Benny would no longer be able to make independent decisions, since investors who purchased BeWhite Corporation stocks would own a certain percentage of the business and have demands that could be ignored.

- More time would need to be devoted to dealing with the Securities and Exchange Commission (SEC)[31] regulations and additional reporting that came with being public.

Disregarding Simon's advice, which would one day cause them trouble, Benny and Paul decided to go ahead with the IPO. The two most influential arguments

---

31 The US Securities and Exchange Commission, is responsible for regulating the stock and options exchanges.

in favour of their decision were the pressure of their competition going public too and their not-so-healthy financial situation. After six months of intensive work, led by Stuart and with the support of Morgan Stanley investment banking division, BeWhite Corporation went public on the New York Stock Exchange (NYSE) on 18 August 1970. The company sold 21,500,000 shares of common stock (60 per cent of the company) at a starting price of $17.28 per share, raising $371 million. Expectations were so high that at the end of the opening day the share price had risen to $32.01, almost double the initial price. BeWhite Corporation was worth more than $1,147 million.

In the days following the IPO the management was flying high and because of Benny's charisma and excellent reputation there was extensive coverage in the business press and on the radio. Every single employee was proud of working for BeWhite Corporation.

Paul and Stuart were impressed by the fact that the IPO project was so successful. In fact, it was the first time that a project had been delivered exactly on the originally established due date and they wanted to share this with their colleagues at the PMI. Benny was very emotional; he never thought that the little business selling spare parts that he had started almost 60 years ago in an old hut close to his home would have reached such prominence and value. He recalled the great people he had met over the years and was thankful to all of them. But Benny was feeling very tired, although he did not mention this to anyone.

On a cold and sunny morning in 1973, Benny died peacefully at the age of 81. His funeral was attended by thousands of employees, chief executives from the top American companies, academics and his family. *Time* magazine featured him on the cover of its April 1973 issue, paying tribute to Benny White's life and achievements. Paul was amazed to see how many people truly appreciated his father. The dean of Harvard Business School, by then a close friend of Benny, presented the closing eulogy:

> *Dear Benny, today is a sad day for all of us: It is not every day that we have the pleasure of meeting such a wonderful person as you. We will never forget your honest and humble leadership style, which you used to build your state-of-the-art business. I, like many other academics, write about concepts and theories; but you have shown us how to implement them in real life. You have raised the management standards to a level never seen before and have become a role model for future*

business leaders throughout the world. We will remain always grateful to you for what you have taught us. Rest in peace, and you will be forever in our minds.

There were no better words to express what all of Benny's friends were thinking.

Benny's death was a big shock to the entire organization. The management board appointed Paul White as his father's successor, and he immediately sent a personal message to all employees telling them that Benny would want them to keep working and enjoying what they do. The message had a powerful effect and soon all BeWhite Corporation's businesses were back on track.

During the second half of the 1970s, the US government deregulated numerous industries, including airlines and railroads, which benefited some of the BeWhite Corporation businesses, especially Spare Parts 20th Century. At the same time, however, the economy entered a period of 'stagflation.'[32] Consumers began to expect continually rising prices, so they bought more. This increased demand pushed up prices, leading to demands for higher wages, which pushed prices higher still in a continuing upward spiral. The government's ever-rising need for funds swelled the budget deficit and led to greater government borrowing, which in turn pushed up interest rates and increased costs for businesses and consumers even further. With energy costs and interest rates high, business investment languished and unemployment rose to uncomfortable levels. This situation had a negative effect on the sales and operating costs of Medical Labs and Constructions Benny. The business that was doing best was C-Transistors, as transistors had become key components in practically all modern electronic devices. Once again, Benny had anticipated the next big business trend.

BeWhite Corporation – Coup d'Etat

In an attempt to slow the pace of high rates of inflation and increasing unemployment, the US Federal Reserve Board refused to supply the additional money that the economy required. This decision caused interest rates to rise, with the result that consumer spending and business borrowing slowed abruptly. The economy soon fell into a deep recession that continued to 1982, when business bankruptcies rose by 50 per cent over the previous year. BeWhite

---

32 'Stagflation' is an economic situation characterized by continuing inflation and stagnant business activity, together with an increasing unemployment rate.

Corporation was hit by this recession, but Paul and his management team were confident that the economy would soon bounce back. But in the winter of 1983, exactly ten years after the death of BeWhite Corporation's founder, Benny White, a major turnaround took place. The board of management decided to remove Paul White from the chief executive role and to nominate Roy McCarthy as the corporation's new CEO. Roy had an exceptional track record: He graduated with high honours from Harvard Business School, spent five years as a principal at McKinsey and had seven years' experience with General Electric. The board felt that Paul's management style was too collaborative and not suitable for the current challenging times. BeWhite Corporation's share price had remained steady at around $17 for the previous three years and the board thought that a radical change was necessary. In a succinct message sent to the press and the SEC, the board stated that it was time for a new management approach.

Paul found out that he had been replaced via a phone call from Stuart Miles, who had read it on the front page of the *Wall Street Journal*. It was a total surprise to both of them, although being publicly quoted had caused some changes in the composition of the corporation's shareholders. In fact, one large hedge fund had become the largest shareholder.

BeWhite Corporation was not the only company to experience such changes. During the early 1980s, 'corporate raiders' bought various corporations whose stock prices were depressed, with the objective of restructuring them either by selling off some of their operations or by dismantling them piece by piece. Looking back, Paul felt that he should have noticed the risk of this happening and bought back part of BeWhite Corporation's stock; but now it was too late. He felt extremely guilty, especially thinking about the pain that this situation would have caused his father. Paul deeply regretted having followed Simon Berkowitz's advice and having pushed his father to bring the company public.

On 1 June 1983, Roy McCarthy became the first CEO of BeWhite Corporation who was not a member of the White family. In his initial speech to employees he announced that in 100 days he would present a turnaround plan to triple the share price in less than five years. The chief executives of the individual companies and the rest of the management team were not involved, other than having a one-hour meeting with the head partner at McKinsey and one of his assistants. In addition, the output of the strategic exercise performed some years ago was completely disregarded – probably because it was administered by a different strategic consulting firm. The whole exercise was driven almost exclusively by Roy and the consultants.

One hundred days later, Roy met with his management team to present the plan. Interestingly, Roy was the youngest in the room and this was the first time a younger CEO had had to supervise older managers, something that they had to get used to going forward. Roy very enthusiastically announced the highlights of the plan:

- 'Spare Parts 20th Century will be sold. I believe that the spare parts market is mature, that margins are very low, and that this division is not prestigious enough for the new BeWhite Corporation I have in mind.'

- 'Parts of Constructions Benny, C-Transistors, and Medical Labs will also be sold. These three businesses are too expensive to run, and they are wasting a lot of money. As a result of these sales, several thousand employees will be laid off. The result will be a 50 per cent decrease in operating costs in three years.'

- 'We want to grow YourMoney into one of the largest banks in the world, providing financial services and advice to large corporations, institutions, medium-sized companies and individuals. It will be the bank for everyone everywhere.'

- 'Half of the money we will make from the sales will be distributed to the shareholders and the other half will be spent acquiring businesses with higher margins and in more prestigious sectors.'

The management team was astonished and unable to express in words what they were feeling, but it was not good. After five minutes of silence, Michael Clark stood up and said what everybody around the table was thinking: that in one go, Roy was going to destroy the company and erase all that Benny had spent so much effort building. Roy McCarthy smiled and said that there was nothing to discuss: 'If someone doesn't believe in my plan, the door is open.'

During the following years, BeWhite Corporation benefited from the rebound of the economy and the beginning of a sustainable period of low inflation and economic growth. The fact that the businesses were doing better had a positive impact on share price, which increased 20 per cent since Roy's arrival. Roy was extremely proud and told everybody that it was thanks to him that the increase was achieved. The board of management and the key shareholders were pleased as well. Roy was featured in *Forbes* magazine as one of the best business leaders of the 1980s. But apart from downsizing two of the businesses, none of Roy's promised changes or objectives were actually achieved. In fact, no concrete projects were derived from his strategic plans; but no one noticed that important flaw.

Every fortnight, Paul had dinner with Stuart Miles, who had been appointed by Roy McCarthy as BeWhite Corporation's head of corporate business development, mergers and acquisitions. The title was really fancy, but it was not really clear what he had to do. In fact, he had no direct line with the chief executives of the five businesses so he was not too busy and had time to think. At each of their dinners, Paul and Stuart spoke about the past, 'the good old days, Benny and how much damage Roy McCarthy was doing to the empire that had taken so much effort to build.

The Years on the Dark Side

Despite not having a job, Paul had enough money to live. He decided not to waste time and instead to follow some late-developed passions: teaching and research. He became a visiting professor of project management at Thunderbird Business School and began serving on the board of the PMI as he was considered one of the country's key project management experts. Once in a while he did some charity work, acting as a management consultant to small enterprises.

But Paul dedicated most of his time to thinking about business, particularly strategy and the link between strategy, projects and operations. He had found the meeting with Igor Ansoff – where the passion for excellence was first discussed – totally enlightening. Paul now saw similarities with his father and understood why Benny had taken him to the meeting with Igor: to awaken his curiosity and passion to find out why things happen in business; to search for excellence; and to help create a better-managed business environment.

In the summer of 1986, Paul drove his four-cylinder Ford Thunderbird to Harvard Business School to meet with Michael Porter, Professor of the Microeconomics of Competiveness and already recognized as the father of modern strategy and a leading authority on the competitiveness and economic development of nations. Michael had admired Paul's father, Benny, and regretted his passing away. Michael explained that his research focused on how a firm or a region can develop a competitive strategy and build a competitive advantage. He first presented the concept of the value chain, which he quickly sketched on the chalkboard:

> *Without going into too much detail, the value chain is the sequence of activities within a company that create value. Products pass through the primary activities of the chain in order, and at each activity the product gains some value. The chain of activities gives the products more added value than the sum of added values of all activities. Besides the primary activities, there are support activities. The whole concept can be used for capturing the value generated along the chain and finding ways of improving the company's business model.*

Paul was impressed by the simplicity of the approach; it seemed so obvious. Michael had a little smile on his face. He then proceeded to explain his concept of the five forces, which is a framework for industry analysis and strategy development. Michael erased the value chain from the chalkboard and drew a square in the middle, representing competitive rivalry within the industry, with four boxes pointing to it. The square in the middle corresponded to the intensity of competitive rivalry. Each box represented a force that determines the competitive intensity and therefore the attractiveness of a market:

1.   The power of customers.

2.   The power of suppliers.

3.   The threat of substituted products.

4.   The potential entry of new competitors.

The five-force model should be used as a qualitative evaluation of a company's strategic position or when considering entering a new market. Once again, the description was clear and the utility of the framework enormous.

   The last takeaway that Michael shared with Paul was his view that companies commonly use three generic types of strategies to achieve and maintain their competitive advantage: cost leadership, differentiation (both broad market scope) and market segmentation (narrow market scope).

Paul took notes, asked several questions and briefly explained his latest views on strategy execution. The topics and discussion were so interesting that he could have spent hours deliberating with Michael. Paul thanked him, promised to keep in touch and drove back home.

That same evening, at their regular dinner, Paul briefed Stuart Miles on his encounter with Michael Porter. In return, Stuart shared the latest developments within BeWhite Corporation: Roy McCarthy had found a buyer for Spare Parts 20th Century. Apparently, one of General Electric's main suppliers was interested in the acquisition. The news felt like a punch in the stomach to Paul, and Stuart said that the news had saddened the entire management team. The four businesses were not doing well either, but Roy seemed convinced that with the sale of Spare Parts they would be transformed. Stuart also mentioned that every year the corporation was starting more projects than they were finishing, but no one seemed to notice.

Over the following years, the situation became worse and worse for BeWhite Corporation. Spare Parts 20th Century was sold hastily and the money made was spent mainly on bonuses and a private company jet. YourMoney, Roy's big bet, filed for Chapter 11 (a US form of bankruptcy) after their ill-considered strategy of providing easy loans and investing in the capital markets doomed them to failure. None of the three businesses was market leader; nor did they have a clear vision or defined strategy. The situation was chaotic. In a panic-driven attempt to find new ways of making money and increasing share price, Roy began to invest in almost any idea presented to him. There was little thought behind his actions and the chief executives of BeWhite Corporation's businesses joined him in his desperate attempts. The situation quickly got out of control and, in 1996, BeWhite Corporation's share price plunged to historical lows.

Paul's Return to BeWhite Corporation

Despite Roy McCarthy's failure to meet his objectives, he did not want to leave the CEO role. In fact, he never admitted that he had failed. He blamed the markets and the external world. He also suspected that some people on his management team did not want him to succeed. But Roy was a survivor and one of his key skills was politics. Despite the fact that BeWhite Corporation's share price had steadily decreased since Roy joined as CEO, he had managed to retain his position for years. His speeches were inspirational and he easily convinced many of the employees that the future was going to be much better and that the failure was not his fault.

But Roy's actions indicated that he had never been interested in the details of any of the businesses. This was totally the opposite of Benny's and Paul's management style, which involved immersing themselves in all facets of each business and discussing them with their management teams. Roy's main goal now was to stay on as CEO for as long as possible, and he viewed anyone who did not support him as an enemy he needed to fight. One morning, Michael Clark, the CFO, told him that selling Spare Parts 20th Century had been a terrible mistake. Roy fired him straight away. The other managers became afraid of Roy and avoided any type of discussion with him. Even the chairman of the board did not dare to confront him. Roy surrounded himself with a few loyal employees who always said what he wanted to hear and with many strategic consultants, who prepared his speeches.

In some divisions, people like Roy became very strong. Using similar skills, they spread this appalling culture throughout the BeWhite Corporation, killing the passion and the motivation to innovate. From 1992 until 1998, the company survived only through fear and inertia, but it was on the verge of bankruptcy. Despite the good performance in the overall economy of the 1990s, BeWhite Corporation's share price dropped again, below the $2 mark; it had become almost 'penny stock.' Roy had managed to erode 90 per cent of the company's value in 15 years as CEO.

The board of management had no doubts this time and fired Roy McCarthy. They asked Paul White to replace him as CEO of BeWhite Corporation, the company his father had started 88 years earlier. Paul needed some time to reflect and had serious doubts about whether to accept the board's request, but he ultimately decided that declining would be like saying no to his father. Besides, after 16 years of teaching and meeting management gurus, Paul now had the opportunity to put in place all his learning and the theories that he had developed.

In September 1998, Paul White became CEO of BeWhite Corporation for the second time. On his first day back, the entire management team and headquarters staff welcomed him with a 15-minutes standing ovation. Paul was deeply touched. He thanked everyone and asked for their support in repairing all the damage that had been done. He promised to return the company to a state that would have made Benny White proud.

Shortly later, Paul gathered the management team and chief executives of the remaining businesses. He appointed Stuart as his deputy and proposed bringing back Michael Clark as CFO. During the meeting, Paul explained that they did not have much time to save the company and that he needed them to commit themselves to turning the situation around. He acknowledged that it would be tough but told the management team that he had total faith in them. Quarterly meetings, which Roy had cancelled, were restored and Paul proposed that until the end of the year they meet on a monthly basis. Paul also promised that by the next meeting he would have a plan to discuss with them.

Paul asked Stuart to thoroughly evaluate the real issues and opportunities at BeWhite Corporation by spending time with the chief executive of each business and also by meeting with employees from the plants and different support offices.

Two weeks later, Stuart's report was lying on Paul's desk. It was succinct and to the point. The situation was worse than Paul had imagined, with the most dramatic concerns being:

Lack of Strategy

BeWhite Corporation had no vision, no mission statement, no strategic plan, no product or market strategy and no strategic planning department. The last strategic plan, which proved to be a total disaster, was drafted by Roy after his 100-day tenure. Each of the remaining three businesses had something written, but it was far from being a strategic plan. It was obvious that the businesses were running without clear direction.

Weak Financial Performance

The financial situation was in dire straits. C-Transistors was the only business making a profit, but this profit was used to cover the losses of Medical Labs and Constructions Benny. Employees had been fired, and the quality of the products and services had decreased dramatically. Sales for the corporation had dropped by more than 60 per cent. Making things worse was the fact that, in his last years, Roy had borrowed large amount of money to invest in new initiatives. BeWhite Corporation was now overleveraged and had to pay large amounts of interest to the banks every month. This overleverage was one of the main reasons why BeWhite Corporation was close to bankruptcy.

Organizational Overlaps and Internal Competition

The organizational structure was not aligned at all to the future needs of BeWhite Corporation. The decentralized model was implemented more than

50 years ago and had not been adapted since. In addition, there were strong overlaps between the operational activities and the projects activities. This misalignment and overlap, together with the aggressive culture that Roy had implemented, created lots of internal competition, even reaching the point where one sale could be claimed by four different salesmen and their managers.

Lack of Execution Culture

There was a total lack of execution in the organization. Due to enormous pressure from Roy to deliver results, management was focusing all their attention on short-term commercial objectives. The lack of strategic plan and priorities for each business meant that employees were doing only what was urgent. In turn, management avoiding making decisions through fear of making mistakes and being censured. The organization was paralysed. There were many good ideas for new products, especially in Medical Labs, but nobody dared mention them to Roy. In C-Transistors, several very interesting acquisitions were studied; but no one dared execute them for fear of being fired.

Unhappy, Unengaged and Unmotivated Staff

Probably the saddest point for Paul in Stuart's report was the fact that staff were unhappy, unengaged and unmotivated. When Benny was at the helm the organization felt like one big family, with everyone enjoying working together and helping each other. But when Roy took over he started firing people and the company fell into a deep depression: motivation and passion had been replaced by fear and disarray.

Unbalanced Distribution of Resources

The allocation of resources, budgets and staff was heavily oriented toward operational tasks. Even though it was the end of the twentieth century, most resources were still used for the operations component of the business. On the other hand, lots of projects were being handled simultaneously by only a handful of employees. There was something wrong with this situation, which Stuart could not explain clearly.

Mismanaged and Misaligned Portfolio of Projects

In the last five years there had been a huge increase in the number of projects. Although it was impossible to know how many projects were running at the time of Stuart's analysis, the estimate was more than 400 projects at an investment of approximately $1 billion. What worried Stuart was that there was no tracking of project status; no clarity about the value they would bring; and no prioritization, which meant that employees themselves decided where to work. This situation was made worse by the fact that Roy was so desperate to create additional sources of value that he wasted substantial funds on useless projects and created such a negative environment that good projects from bright people were never brought forward.

Total Lack of Focus

Paul concluded that the company had lost its focus, the key competency that Benny White had transmitted to all his employees from the days of Spare Parts Benny through to the creation of BeWhite Corporation. Apart from Roy's obvious contribution to this *lack of focus*, something else became clear to Paul. During his years teaching and researching, Paul noticed that over the last 50 years or so, companies had been taking on more and more projects – at a rate of one or two extra every year – while most improvements concentrated on the operations side of the business. Two different dimensions were emerging in every organization and two different ways of managing were colliding, creating tensions and pulling against each other. In a sense, this ruthless trend was pushing the organization to be *unfocused* as well, thus accelerating the company's degradation and loss of shareholder value. Paul could not define all this with precision and was unable to clearly identify the symptoms of such a trend; but when he saw Stuart's report everything became clear. The consequences of this trend were lying on his desk.

It was obvious that if Paul wanted to turn the organization around he had to find a method or framework that had never been seen before in the world of management. He took a few days off to try to get inspiration from the notes he had taken at his meetings with the management guru, from all his readings and from his own ideas.

BeWhite Corporation Becomes a FOCUSED Organization

After much thought Paul realized that BeWhite Corporation was most successful when it demonstrated the following seven characteristics:

1. *Fewer projects and products*. Most of the corporation's value had been created when it was running just a few projects, such as the

standardization project or the integration into Spare Parts 20th Century. Linked to the importance of taking on fewer projects was the need to generate fewer products, as Henry Ford had advised Paul's father.

2. *Organized staff.* When Benny was around, everybody knew what they had to do – always in the area in which they excelled. Employees were recognized for their work. In addition, the organization found the right balance between operations and projects.

3. *Competitive mindset.* Despite the fact that Benny was not what you would call a 'tough guy,' he was determined to beat the competition. Innovation was one of the keys to success and Benny was always aware of the latest market trends to anticipate the competition – evidenced, for example, by his decision to acquire Aircraft Parts Inc. During the more than 60 years of Benny's leadership there was never the slightest hint of internal competition. Team spirit was part of the organization's DNA.

4. *Urgency.* With a soft but persuasive approach, Benny instilled a sense of urgency in the mindset of his managers and employees. This technique was important to get the workers' full attention and best efforts. Benny did not always use this approach but he did know when it was needed and how it should be employed.

5. *Strategic alignment.* For many decades, Benny's businesses lacked an explicit strategy, yet every initiative that Benny invested in was linked to his vision and strategic goal of expanding or improving the business. Looking back, the first initiatives were probably not the best-managed projects, as they were unexplored territory; but they were always prioritized and had Benny's attention.

6. *Excellence.* One characteristic that comes across all the time in Benny's management style is his passion for excellence. Since his early days, when he was producing cylinders and valve gears for trains, his products were already of the highest standard. His attention to detail was remarkable; and it was not only on the production side: he truly cared about his customers. Benny transmitted this obsession with quality and continuous improvements to all his employees.

7.   *Discipline.* Benny may not have been in the army but he had enormous respect and appreciation for some of its techniques – notably discipline. He understood the importance of discipline at work to get the best out of people. Although in the early days his management style was somewhat directive, he was never bossy. Even when he learned to lead his managers and employees in a collaborative way, he ensured that there was discipline throughout. In fact, when he was young he very quickly noticed that most of the successful people were extremely disciplined, so Benny first applied discipline to himself.

Benny's son Paul recognized that what he had to do to make BeWhite Corporation *focused* again was to concentrate on those areas at which Benny thought his company would excel. Business success and employee satisfaction would follow from there. This realization was so simple, and Paul felt totally enlightened. Paul shared his thinking with Stuart, who was amazed by the clarity of the rationale and the simplicity of the framework. Together, and based on decades of experience in project management, they developed a unique approach to turn the company into a focused organization. They called this approach an 'accelerated transformation project.'

For this project, which was launched in March 1999, there was no need to create a burning platform because all management was fully committed and aware of the importance of this change. Against all the odds and experts' concerns, BeWhite Corporation completed the turnaround in only nine months. A clear strategy was defined and priorities had been communicated to all employees: C-Transistors and Medical Lab were to become the new core businesses and would focus on innovation, while Constructions Benny would expand internationally. The organizational structure was reviewed and aligned to support both operational and project activities. A strategy execution office was established and an investment decision and strategy execution committee was appointed to oversee all investments and the execution of the strategy. Many projects were cancelled and only those that were relevant and linked to the agreed-upon strategy were kept. Momentum was created and important benefits were quickly evident. BeWhite Corporation was again *focused* and back in the black too. Most important, the employees recovered their joy and passion for their work.

The accelerated transition project was so different yet so successful that Stuart and Paul received an award from the PMI for the best-run project of 1999.

The award recognized a project team for superior performance and exemplary project management in the execution of a project. Since its launch in 1989 the award had always been given to large engineering and construction projects.[33] This was the first time that the award had gone to a transformation project, which made Paul and Stuart extremely proud.

Having turned the organization around, there was one last thing that Paul needed to complete before he was at peace. He took two weeks off, knowing that the company was in the right hands with Stuart in the lead, and started to write the first chapter of a book that he wanted to dedicate to his father. This book would deal with Benny's achievements and the new theories that he had developed over the years. The book would be called *The Focused Organization*.

---

33 The first award of project of the year was given to the Delta Airlines Terminal 5 expansion project.

Bibliography

Aaltonen, P. and Ikävalko, H., Implementing strategies successfully, *Integrated Manufacturing Systems*, 13(6), 415–18 (2002).

Ansoff, H.I., Strategies for diversification, *Harvard Business Review*, 35(5), 113–24 (September–October 1957).

Ansoff, H.I., *Corporate Strategy*. New York: McGraw-Hill (1965).

Axson, D.A.J., The fastest route to right answers: Refining approaches for better decision-making through performance reporting, *Strategy & Leadership*, 27(3), 6–10 (1999).

Barrows, E., What is strategy execution? *American Management Association* [online, 7 January 2010]. Available at: http://www.amanet.org/training/articles/What-Is-Strategy-Execution.aspx [accessed 24 November 2011].

Birnik, A. and Moat, R., Developing actionable strategy, *Business Strategy Review*, 19(1), 28–33 (Spring 2008).

Bossidy, L. and Charan, R., *Execution: The Discipline of Getting Things Done*. New York: Crown Business (2002).

Chandler, A., *Strategy and Structure: Chapters in the History of the American Industrial Enterprise*. Cambridge, MA: MIT Press (1962).

De Wit, B. and Meyer, R., *Strategy Synthesis: Resolving Strategy Paradoxes to Create Competitive Advantage*. Andover: Cengage Learning (2010).

Deming, W.E., *Out of the Crisis*. Cambridge, MA: MIT Press (2000).

Drucker, P., *Concept of the Corporation*. New York: John Day (1946).

Drucker, P., *The Practice of Management*. New York: Harper Paperbacks (2006 [1954]).

Ford, H., *My Life and Work*. Champaign, IL: Book Jungle (2007 [1922]).

Franken, A., Edwards, C. and Lambert, R., Executing strategic change: Understanding the critical management elements that lead to success, *California Management Review*, 51(3), 49–73 (Spring 2009).

Hamel, G. and Prahalad, C.K., *Competing for the Future*. Boston, MA: Harvard Business School Press (1996).

Hammer, M., Reengineering work: Don't automate, obliterate, *Harvard Business Review*, 104–12 (July–August 1990).

Hammer, M. and Champy, J., *Reengineering the Corporation: A Manifesto for Business Revolution*. New York: HarperBusiness (2003).

Hrebiniak, L.G., *Making Strategy Work: Leading Effective Execution and Change*. Upper Saddle River, NJ: Wharton School Publishing (2005).

Isaacson, W., *Steve Jobs*. New York: Simon & Schuster (2011).

Kahney, L., *Inside Steve's Brain: Business Lessons from Steve Jobs, the Man who Saved Apple*. London: Atlantic Books (2009).

Kaplan, R. and Norton, D., *The Strategy-Focused Organization: How Balanced Scorecard Companies Thrive in the New Business Environment*. Boston, MA: Harvard Business School Press (2001).

Kaplan, R. and Norton, D., *The Execution Premium: Linking Strategy to Operations for Competitive Advantage*. Boston, MA: Harvard Business School Press (2008).

Katzenbach, J. and Smith, D., *The Wisdom of Teams: Creating the High-Performance Organization*. Maidenhead: McGraw-Hill (2003).

Kelly, E.J. and Walker, M.R., Critical Path Planning and Scheduling. Proceedings of the Eastern Joint Computer Conference, Boston, MA (March 1959).

Kotter, J.P., *Leading Change*. Boston, MA: Harvard Business School Press (1996).

Kruger, D. and Ramphal, R., *Operations Management*. Cape Town: Oxford University Press (2nd edn, 2009).

Levine, H., *Project Portfolio Management: A Practical Guide to Selecting Projects, Managing Portfolios, and Maximizing Benefits*. San Francisco: Jossey-Bass (2005).

Mankins, M.C. and Steele, R., Turning great strategy into great performance, *Harvard Business Review*, 83(7), 64–72 (July–August 2005).

Martin, R.L., The execution trap: Drawing a line between strategy and execution almost guarantees failure, *Harvard Business Review*, 88(7–8), 64–71 (July–August 2010).

Mintzberg, H., *The Rise and Fall of Strategic Planning*. New York: Free Press (1994).

Mintzberg, H., Ahlstrand, B. and Lampel, J., *Strategy Safari: A Guided Tour Through the Wilds of Strategic Management*. New York: Free Press (2005).

Moenaert, R.K., Robben, H.S.J. and Gouw, P., *Marketing, Strategy & Organization: Building Sustainable Business*. Leuven: Lannoo Campus (2010).

Moore, S., *Strategic Project Portfolio Management: Enabling a Productive Organization*. Hoboken, NJ: Wiley (2009).

Peters, T. and Waterman, R. Jr, *In Search of Excellence: Lessons from America's Best-Run Companies*. New York: HarperBusiness (2004 [1982]).

Porter, M.E., What is strategy? *Harvard Business Review*, 74(6), 61–78 (November–December 1996).

Porter, M.E., *Competitive Advantage: Creating and Sustaining Superior Performance*. New York: Free Press (1985).

Porter, M.E., *Competitive Strategy: Techniques for Analyzing Industries and Competitors*. New York: Free Press (1998).

Prahalad, C.K. and Hamel, G., The core competence of a corporation, *Harvard Business Review*, 68(3), 79–91 (May–June 1990).

Raps, A., Strategy implementation: An insurmountable obstacle? *Handbook of Business Strategy*, 6(1), 141–6 (2005).

Rothman, J., *Manage Your Project Portfolio: Increase Your Capacity and Finish More Projects*. Raleigh, NC: The Pragmatic Programmers (2009).

Sanwal, A., *Optimizing Corporate Portfolio Management*. Chichester: John Wiley & Sons (2007).

Steve Jobs: The *Rolling Stone* Interview (4 April 1996).

Taylor, F.W., *The Principles of Scientific Management*. New York: Cosimo Classics (2010 [1911]).

Index

If you have found this book useful you may be interested in other titles from Gower

Project Politics
A Systematic Approach to Managing Complex Relationships
Nita A. Martin
Hardback: 978-0-566-08895-7
e-book: 978-1-4094-1261-8

Project Success
Critical Factors and Behaviours
Emanuel Camilleri
Hardback: 978-0-566-09228-2
e-book: 978-0-566-09229-9

Tame, Messy and Wicked Risk Leadership
David Hancock
Paperback: 978-0-566-08806-3
e-book: 978-1-4094-0873-4

Making the Business Case:
Proposals that Succeed for Projects that Work
Ian Gambles
Paperback: 978-0-566-08745-5
e-book: 978-0-7546-9427-4

Benefit Realisation Management
A Practical Guide to Achieving Benefits Through Change
Gerald Bradley
Hardback: 978-1-4094-0094-3
e-book: 978-1-4094-1086-7

GOWER

Communicating Strategy
Phil Jones
Paperback: 978-0-566-08810-0
e-book: 978-0-7546-8288-2

Enterprise Growth Strategy
Vision, Planning and Execution
Dhirendra Kumar
Hardback: 978-0-566-09198-8
e-book: 978-0-566-09199-5

Gower Handbook of Internal Communication
Edited by Marc Wright
Hardback: 978-0-566-08689-2
e-book: 978-0-7546-9097-9

MisLeadership
John Rayment and Jonathan Smith
Hardback: 978-0-566-09226-8
e-book: 978-0-566-09227-5

Project-Oriented Leadership
Ralf Müller and J Rodney Turner
Hardback: 978-0-566-08923-7
e-book: 978-1-4094-0939-7

Visit **www.gowerpublishing.com** and

- search the entire catalogue of Gower books in print
- order titles online at 10% discount
- take advantage of special offers
- sign up for our monthly e-mail update service
- download free sample chapters from all recent titles
- download or order our catalogue

Printed in the United States
by Baker & Taylor Publisher Services